Designing for Empathy

The Architecture of Connections in Learning Environments

Aybars Aşçı

Contributing essay by Dr. Julia Higdon

APPLIED RESEARCH +DESIGN PUBLISHING

CONTENTS

1

DESIGNING FOR EMPATHY

I INTRODUCTION

In 2016, I was invited to meet the leadership team of a pre-K through 12th grade school. They asked me to become their "global design architect," collaborating on multiple campuses that were at different stages of development. Since then, the complexity of the design challenges we have been tackling has varied from large-scale campus planning to furniture design. During our research, the discussions we had with educators repeatedly touched on one key concept: empathy.

In development theory, the importance of empathy is frequently emphasized, but in architectural discourse empathy is much less studied. One reason may be, as architecture theorist Juhani Pallasmaa argues, that "geometric configurations are easier to imagine than the shapeless and dynamic acts of life and the ephemeral feelings evoked by architecture."[1] The origins of the discussions of empathy in architecture, however, can be traced back to the nineteenth-century German philosophy of aesthetics, where the concept of empathy originated.[2]

The term *Einfühlung*—translated as "feeling into"—was coined in the early 1870s by philosopher Robert Vischer in his dissertation on emotional projection.[3] According to Vischer, Einfühlung describes unconscious projections of the body and soul into the form of the object.[4] For instance, according to Vischer, the pleasure we take from observing horizontal lines—for example, watching the horizon—is related to the horizontal position of our eyes, or similarly, our appreciation of symmetry is because it is analogous to our body.[5] A few decades later, Theodor Lipps popularized a psychological

1.1 (Facing page) Avenues Shenzhen Early Learning Center theory of Einfühlung.[6] Lipps expanded the concept beyond the experience of inanimate objects or physical environments to understand the mental states of other people.[7] The translation of Einfühlung to English language as "empathy" first appeared at the beginning of twentieth century, almost simultaneously, in Vernon Lee's book on aesthetics and in Edward Bradford Titchener's lectures on psychology.[8]

Even though the word empathy is only just over a century old, it has developed into multiple definitions and proliferated into various interpretations across disciplines. Especially with the recent empirical evidence emerging from neuroscience, the notion of empathy has become increasingly popular, which has resulted in a surge of publications covering this in the past two decades.

In this book, empathy and its importance in the design of learning environments is dissected across three conceptual threads. The first thread springs from the original philosophical theory of empathy in aesthetics, which focuses on the phenomenological immediacy of our aesthetic appreciation of objects and environment.[9] Learning environments exist within social, cultural, and environmental contexts, and therefore, the specifics of these contexts play an active role in the development of human beings. Context is not a mere vessel that is impartial to the life that takes place within it. Likewise, architecture is not a mere shelter. According to Christian Norberg-Schulz, each space carries a distinct character, which he references as the "genius loci" (the spirit of place) and, by extension, "the task of the architect is to create meaningful places."[10] In other words, placemaking has its own semantics, and when we experience a place, we are also experiencing the narratives embedded in the language of architecture. It is the power of these narratives that can be transformative in the development of empathy. The design conjectures presented in this book are anchored in the experience of architecture and the narratives that emerge from it.

The second conceptual tread of empathy originates from Theodor Lipps's claim that "empathy should be understood as the primary epistemic means of gaining knowledge of other minds."[11] Perspective taking as an empathy development strategy is key in my argument. Transporting perspective taking in empathy from psychology to the perspectival (architectural) space, through the use of projective geometry, is the intellectual hinge of this book.

It is my argument that the forces that operate in our spatial cognition also have the ability to shift perspectives and therefore help us develop empathy. This is what I call the geometry of empathy.

In the field of psychology, two distinct research interests evolved: empathy as an emotional phenomenon and empathy as a cognitive phenomenon.[12] The third conceptual tread of this book highlights the cognitive processes involved with empathy. I highlight the biases channeled through empathy—how emotional contagion can result in discriminatory behavior and how it can lead to violent acts in extreme cases. For instance, bullying in the school yard, or ganging up against one another, are behavior patterns that emerge from in-group/out-group bias. These tendencies are what is often referred to as the "dark side" of empathy.[13] My focus, however, emphasizes the cognitive processes of empathy, instrumental to building a critical mindset to gain knowledge, rather than the strong and occasionally corrosive connections built through emotional contagion.

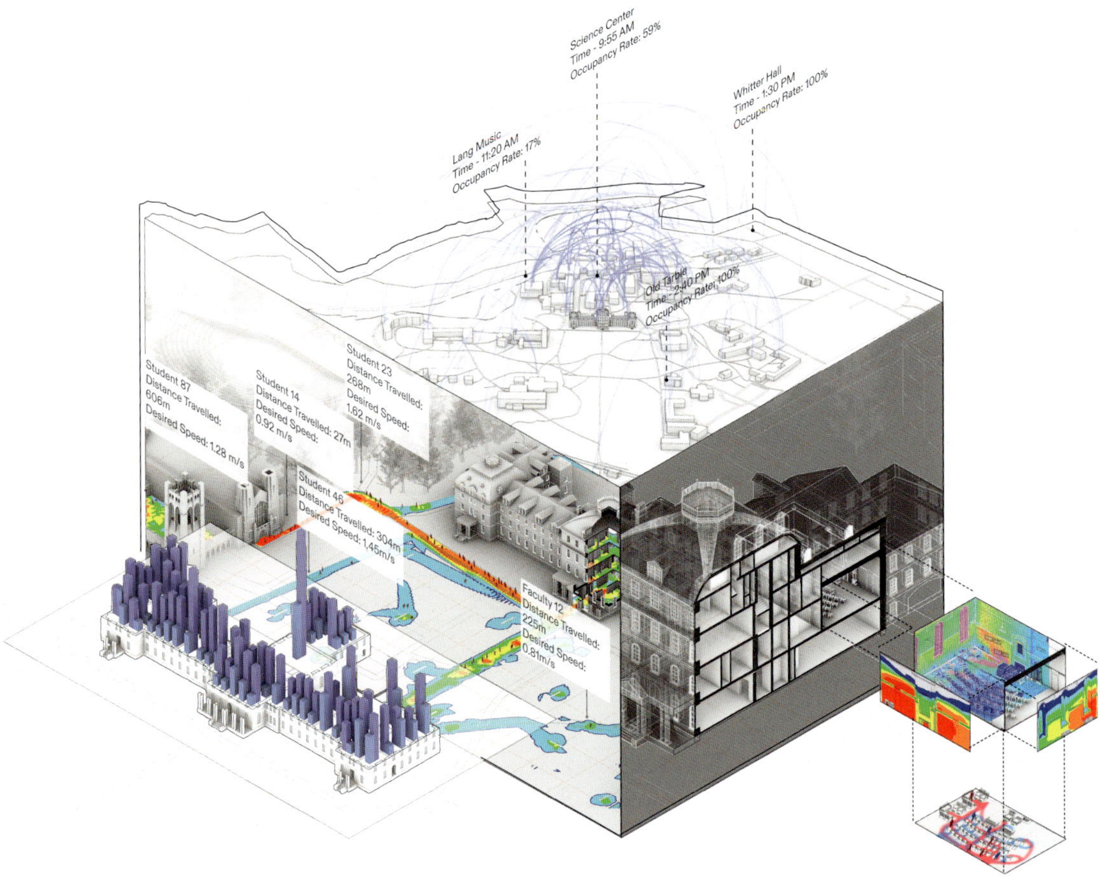

Science Center
Time - 9:55 AM
Occupancy Rate: 59%
Whitter Hall
Time - 1:30 PM
Occupancy Rate: 100%
Lang Music
Time - 11:20 AM
Occupancy Rate: 17%
Old Tarble
Time - 2:40 PM
Occupancy Rate: 100%
Student 23
Distance Travelled:
268m
Desired Speed:
1.62 m/s
Student 87
Distance Travelled:
606m
Desired Speed: 1.28 m/s
Student 14
Distance Travelled: 27m
Desired Speed:
0.92 m/s
Student 46
Distance Travelled: 304m
Desired Speed: 1.45m/s
Faculty 12
Distance Travelled:
225m
Desired Speed:
0.81m/s

II EMPATHY AND DESIGN

Empathy and design can mean vastly different things depending on who the subjects of empathy are and at what point in the design process the discussion on empathy is taking place. For instance, if we are talking about a designer's empathy with the future users of the design, we will be discussing the empathic imagination of the designer, or in other words, the imagination of an architect to feel like the future owner during the design process. Whereas the user's relationship with the design brings into discussion the user experience. This is often referred as empathic design.[14] Another important distinction is the timing of this discussion. In other words: Are we talking about design and empathy during the design process or after the design is complete? Yet again, different subjects in either scenario will generate a different framework of discussion.

We can define two distinct perspectives on empathy and design: empathy in the design process and designing for empathy. In empathy in the design process, we can further distinguish three subcategories: empathic imagination, empathic design, and participatory or co-design.[15]

Empathic Imagination

Throughout the design process, designers can imagine the experiential qualities of spaces by utilizing different modes of representations, such as drawings, models, renderings, or virtual reality simulations. The imagination process can almost be discussed as the architect acting as the future occupant, playing the role and the personalities, like an actor taking on the character in a play, whereby "the designer places him/herself in the role of the future dweller, and tests the validity of the ideas through this imaginative exchange of roles and personalities."[16] Juhani Pallasmaa argues that the empathic imagination works in a way whereby the architect is,

> bound to conceive the design essentially for him/herself as the momentary surrogate of the actual occupant. Without usually being aware of it, the designer turns into a silent actor on the imaginary stage of each project. At the end of the design process, the architect

1.2 (Facing page) Campus connectivity analytics by Efficiency Lab for Architecture.

1.3 Telluride House, Telluride, Colorado

offers the building to the user as a gift. It is a gift in the sense that the designer has given birth to the other's home as a surrogate mother gives birth to the child of someone who is not biologically capable of doing so herself.[17]

In 2016, a New York family asked me to design a vacation house for them in Telluride, Colorado. They wanted to live in a glass house. Like most architects, I imagined building a glass house for myself one day. The empathic imagination of the architect, pretending to be the user—the role play that Pallasmaa describes—comes naturally when designing a glass house nested within a breathtaking canyon. As I sketched the ideas of the house, I imagined living in it. The three cascading glass pavilions would be nested within the steep slope of the mountain, creating viewing platforms expanding toward the panoramic views of the Box Canyon. (Figure **1.4**) The house would become almost like tiered seating for contemplating this majestic environment, and each room in the house would expand toward the exterior, blurring the boundaries of inside and out. (Figure **1.5**)

1.4 Telluride House, Telluride, Colorado

1.5 (Following spread) Telluride House, view toward the box canyon, from the living room. The boundaries between the interior and exterior are blurred.

Shortly after the completion of the project, I received this letter from the owner:

> Seeing this beautiful building is one thing. The lines of snow on the railings and rooftop blend with the striations of snow on the cliffs overhead: it's just as you wanted it to be. But to be in it, to wake up in the middle of the night and to be entirely surrounded (I kept thinking embraced) by the canyon mountains glowing in moonlight topped by brilliant stars, is an experience that even now, on this rainy day in New York, almost brings me to tears. And then in the morning, to see those same mountains, and watch the view change with the sun's position—it defies description. Later, I'd walk outside and look at the footprints of all the animals who visited us in the night—deer, elk, coyotes, rabbits…One day a small herd of mule deer came to visit and grazed their way around the entire house, stopping to look at us in the windows. On other days, a herd of elk would meander up the road past the house. We all found ourselves

> having to stop all the time just to look, to see what we'd be missing if we weren't looking out at nature. This house creates a feeling of being present that is hard to maintain in everyday life.[18]

The satisfaction I felt reading this letter goes beyond the fulfillment of an architect's services to a client, toward the empathic connection between my imaginations and the experience of the owner.

"Before you live in a glass house you do not know how colorful nature is," stated Mies van der Rohe, underlining the phenomenological dimension of being in a glass house.[19] When designing the Telluride House, I imagined that the glass house would create a heightened awareness of being inside this majestic canyon, and from the owner's perspective this translated into a house that "creates a feeling of being present that is hard to maintain in everyday life." According to Pallasmaa's concept of empathic imagination, if my acting of a play character during the design process was the rehearsal, the act of living in the house confirmed the success of the performance.

It is easy to detect the empathic imagination at work here, given the similarities between the aspirations of the owner—to have a glass house nested within a beautiful setting—and the architect's own dream to live in a glass house one day. However, the limitations of the empathic imagination become obvious once the scale and the typology between the architect and the user grows. It is one thing to see empathic imagination at play during a design process of a glass house—a place of desire for people of similar backgrounds—it is another one to conceptualize, for instance, a rehabilitation center for brain injury through empathic imagination. Beyond its limitations, it should be noted that, relying heavily on the empathic imagination as part of the design process has the problematic notion of over-emphasizing the architect's perspective.

Empathic Design

Empathic design differs from empathic imagination in two major ways. Unlike empathic imagination where the focus is on how the designer can imagine themselves as the user during the design process, the focus of empathic design is about how users feel about the design. The second difference with empathic imagination is the role of the designer which, as Koskinen and Battarbee describe, shifts from being a legislator of how the user should or should not feel about the design to becoming an interpreter of user feedback that is collected during the design process.[20] In other words, design decisions are guided by user feedback, and the designer's personal experience and choices are not accounted for or they become less important.

Empathic design is a popular concept in product design, where user experience is tested through engaging user groups with programs such as piloting or prototyping to provide feedback to the design process. The user experience is often understood as how the product creates a meaningful relationship with the user. The emotional intensity can be connected to the user's physical, social, psychological, and ideological relationship with the product. For instance, an ergonomic feature of the product may create a sense of comfort, its social popularity may give a sense of belonging, its color and texture may be calming, and its story of sustainability may align with the user's ethical values.

Unlike product design, prototyping is less applicable to architecture projects, except, perhaps full-scale mock-ups of a repeated component of a large-scale project, such as a single room mock-up in a hotel project. Therefore, the iterative feedback loop with user groups during the design process differs from product design. In the holistic scale of an architectural project, the user experience can only be simulated and analyzed with virtual representation tools.

Participatory Design

Just as empathic design is popular in product design, participatory design is embraced in the planning community, where the design decisions about the public spaces are informed by deep community engagements. The community is brought into the design process, within which they have a voice in design decision making through engagement strategies such as workshops and surveys. Different than empathic design, where the user engages in the process much later (for example, after the first prototype of the product

1.6 Avenues Silicon Valley, section axonometric through the portal Structure. The bridges connect the two academic buildings and the portal structure provides shading for the outdoor learning environments.

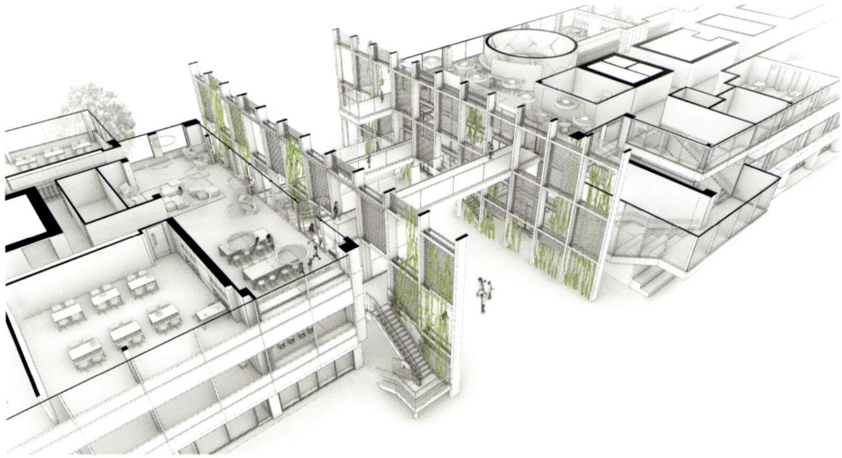

emerges), in participatory design, the user is a part of the design process from the beginning and is encouraged to act like the designer. The community workshops held by planners usually provide drawing and modeling tools to encourage users to express their ideas through sketching, marking up plans, or modifying physical models. If in empathic design the role of the designer shifts from a legislator to an interpreter, in participatory design it becomes the role of the moderator. The designer or planner as moderator, with their experience and technical knowledge, guides the design conversation within which users have an active voice.

Designing for Empathy

In his article "The Empathic Space and Shared Consciousness," Richard Manzotti shifts the focus of discussion on empathy and design (in this case in museums) from the design process to the experience within the design. According to Manzotti, what makes a museum a special place is not the objects it presents, but the connections between the visitors while they are in the presence of these objects. He writes:

> Museums might offer a shared space for developing empathic bonds among visitors. Such a space would not be a physical container of

> items and their curators but rather an "empathic" space of spread consciousness. The objects are not the goal of the museum; they have never been. The objects are the means. The goal of the museum is what happens inside it, in terms of the building of a shared consciousness where empathy is among the key forces at play. The goal of the museums is represented by what happens among its visitors. If visitors had no empathic feelings and went out of the museum unchanged by the presence of other visitor, then the museum would fail.[21]

While discussions on empathy during the design process focus on the role and the mindset of the designer, designing for empathy is about the shared experience of the users after the completion of the design. We should differentiate the shared experience of the users here, from the user experience discussed in empathic design. The focus of empathic design is the experience of the user with a product, system, or service. However, the objective of designing for empathy is not about empathy with the design, but it is how users develop empathy for each other because of the design.

Furthermore, designing for empathy is not limited to humans only. It expands to life that takes place in and around the design in a broader sense; it includes empathy with nature. Architecture involves engaging, transforming, and changing the environment, and thereby it has the power to catalyze empathic relationships between users as well as to develop empathy with nature. This is the focus of *Designing for Empathy: The Architecture of Connections in Learning Environments.*

III ARCHITECTURAL CONJECTURES ON DEVELOPMENTAL PSYCHOLOGY

The idea that architecture can change the world, a conviction popular amongst architects, is the undercurrent of this book. The premise of this conviction gives each architectural project the agency to communicate an idea, which, historically, has encouraged architects to manifest their theories through design. There are many notable examples of this in architectural history such as Le Corbusier's "Modulor," a treatise on proportions in architecture, or his urban vision "The City of Tomorrow." More recently, we can look to Steven Holl's "Urban Condensers," a manifesto on creating profound spatial experiences in public spaces.

In the tradition of architectural research through design, this book investigates how the design of learning environments can influence the development of empathy. Therefore, the projects presented in the following chapters included are not meant to form a monograph of my studio's work, but they present a series of conjectures on designing for empathy. Like Karl Popper's definition of conjectures in scientific theory, the design conjectures in this book are not the digest of observations, but they are inventions, boldly put for trial. As such, they can be tested and refuted.[22]

I have included both finished buildings and projects that are on the boards. The finished projects allowed us to make on-site observations and conduct post-occupancy interviews with user groups to understand their interactions with the spaces. However, it is not the intention or the scope of this book to test the design conjectures through observations, interviews, questionnaires, or any other empathy assessment techniques. My intention is to provoke scholars in the fields of education, sociology, and psychology to test the conjectures put forward here.

1.7 (Facing page) Avenues Miami campus forum.

Navigating the Conjectures

When I first began writing this book, I sat down with Dr. Julia Higdon to discuss the importance of seminal development theories in our design investigations. During our conversations and workshops, Dr. Higdon suggested that we might imagine a triangular map to help position the critical theoretical arguments and their associated vantage points. This idea eventually became a map that situates the theoretical intersections between multiple disciplines as they relate to the design explorations in this book. In other words, the map sets the framework to situate the design conjectures, and for the reader, it is a device to navigate the interdisciplinary connections presented here.

The map is built in three consecutive steps, starting with locating the vantage points of the development theories, then layering in the three critical disciplines, and finally defining a zone of connections between these disciplines and the design conjectures.

Like all maps, this diagram offers both a level of abstraction and specificity. Its abstraction is due to the curated choices on the pieces and parts of theories included as they relate to the framework of the arguments in the book. On the other hand, its specificity relates to its relationship to my design research. In other words, as a map, it functions as a companion to the design conjectures presented in this book.

Map #1

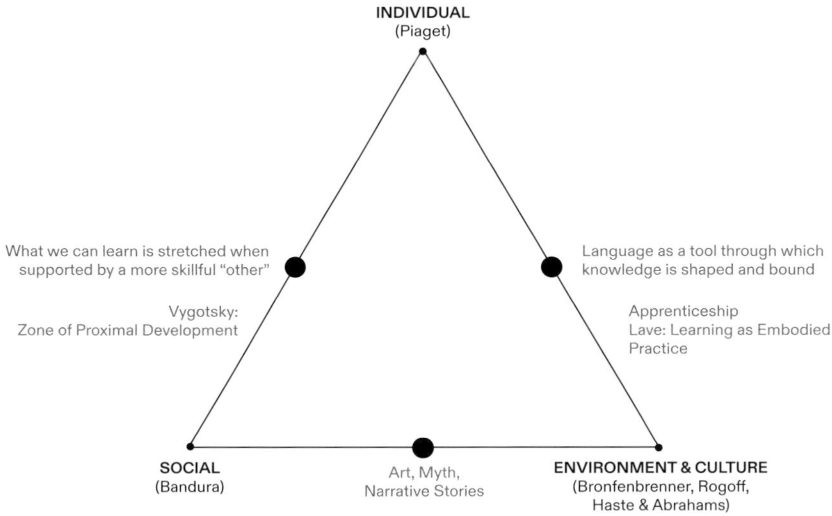

1.8 Map #1

Dr. Higdon describes three vantage points—individual, social, and environment & culture—in her discussion of empathy and development (See page 44). As shown in Figure **1.8**, she proposes a mapping of these vantage points as the three vertices of a triangle.[23] Even though most development theories will not fit into any one of these individual vertices, it is helpful to situate their key focus in relation to the vertices in the diagram. For instance, Jean Piaget's Theory of Cognitive Development (1929) would spring from the vantage point of the individual. According to Piaget, development "is a spontaneous process that comes from the child. It comes from inner maturational growth and, more importantly, from the child's own efforts to make sense of the world."[24]

Albert Bandura's Social Learning Theory (1971), on the other hand, puts the emphasis on learning and social settings. Bandura assessed that "in social situations we often learn much more rapidly simply by observing the behavior of others."[25] Bandura had a strong objection to Piaget's view of development. According to Bandura, "children do not primarily learn on their own, nor does their thinking undergo broad stage transformations."[26] Bandura's theory anchors the "social" vertex of the triangle.

From a third vantage point, Barbara Rogoff stated that "Human development is a cultural process."[27] Her development model (2003) is a fluid process, within which both the context and the individual evolve. For Rogoff, "Humans develop through their changing participation in the socio-cultural activities of their communities, which also change."[28] Helen Haste and Salie Abrahams also highlight increased sophistication in our use of cultural tools, as well as participation and cultural change, as hallmarks of development, in contrast with a perspective that focuses on the development of individual, in-the-head cognition.[29] Their strong emphasis on development and culture locates them on the "environment and culture" vertex of the map.

While the focus of some development theories is strongly biased toward a single vantage point, there are others that negotiate multiple vantage points. For instance, Lev Vygotsky's (1930–1935) development theory emerges from the dialectic relationship between the person's own ability to acquire knowledge or skills and the influence of others. Vygotsky as a dialectic theorist, reconciled these seemingly contradictory positions, by postulating on "what happens when the growing child, trying to figure things out for herself, encounters adults who try to teach her things."[30]

If the vertices of the triangle represent the focus of different vantage points, the edges represent the relationship between these vantage points. Therefore, Vygotsky's development theory is placed on the edge between the "individual" and "social" vertices.

Map #2

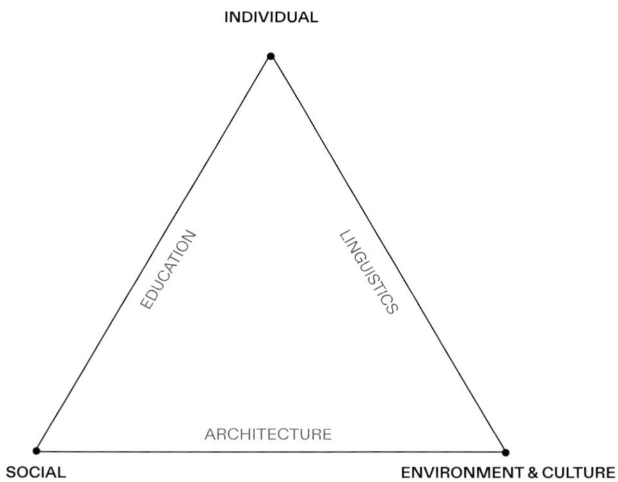

1.9 Map #2

By situating the vantage points of seminal development theories, the first map forms a base layer, establishing the intellectual terrain of my investigations. The second map helps to bridge the development theories with the design conjectures, by locating the three key disciplines—architecture, education, and linguistics—along the edges of the triangle in between relevant vantage points.

One thing to keep in mind is that the vertices still represent the focus points of seminal development theories. In other words, the "individual" vertex does not represent a person, but the vantage point of relevant development theories. Otherwise, it would imply that architecture as a discipline is furthest apart from the individual, which would be a misrepresentation; rather, it is furthest away from Piaget's development theory.

Architecture

What is the influence of architecture on human development? Planners, architects, and designers are responsible in shaping the physical environment, such as homes, schools, cultural and religious centers, neighborhoods,

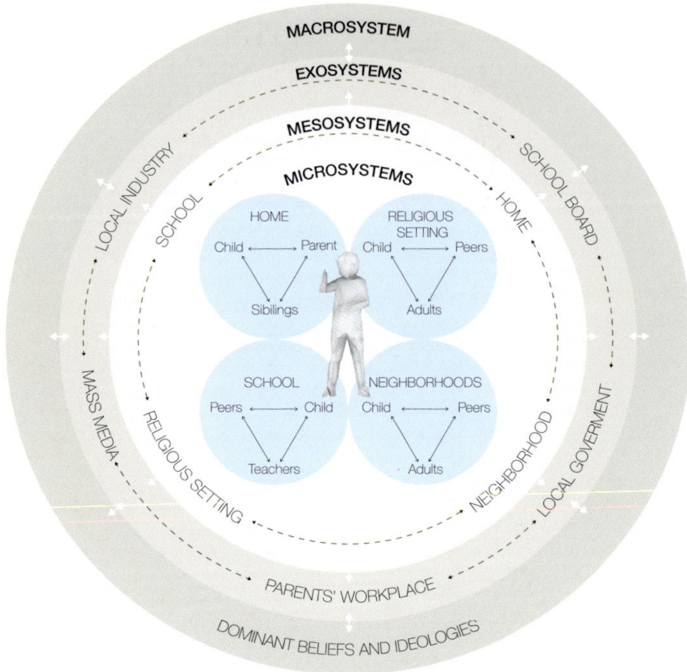

1.10 Urie Bronfenbrenner's nested ecological system as interpreted in Michael Cole and Sheila Cole's textbook, *The Development of Children.*

cities within which human development takes place. However, architecture is conspicuously absent in most development theories, even though the environment is omnipresent.

Let's look at Urie Bronfenbrenner's development model, which is a nested ecological system.[31] (Figure **1.10**) The inner core of his model—the microsystem—defines an individual's immediate experiences, which happen at home, school, religious settings, and the neighborhood. These environments are places of interaction with others and, therefore, where social learning takes place. From the perspective of the built environment, one can write about each of these typologies, identifying in detail the architectural elements and how life within these spaces can be influenced by these elements. Consider, for example, how something infrastructural, like a stove-heated home necessitates social gathering. The stove becomes, both literally and metaphorically, the center of the life in this type of house, and thus social gathering occurs as a necessity. On the other hand, a centrally heated home does not rely on a single focal point for heating, and consequently, the spaces do not gather around a "heart," but they can sprawl. In this type of home, each room can transform into its own autonomous entity, and as a result, it is easier to avoid social contact.

The physical environment is present in development theories that spring from the "environment and culture" vantage point, like the neighborhood in Bronfenbrenner's model. Another example is Jean Lave's apprenticeship model, which she developed through her studies on the workshops located at "Taylor's Ally in Liberia."[32] Lave spent years studying the social dynamics in these workshops, understanding the importance of apprenticeship within the specifics of socio-cultural context, which influenced her ideas on "situated learning." On the contrary, it is harder to see any cues of the physical environment in Piaget's theory, as the development of the individual evolves devoid of any spatial context.

In reference to the vantage point of development theories, architecture is located in the map at the edge between the "social" and "environment and culture" vertices.

Education

What we can learn is expanded when we are supported by a skillful other, which highlights the significance of the teacher and the influence of peers in human development. Therefore, "formal" education is located in between the "individual" and "social" vertices of the triangle. The education edge refers specifically to "schooling" as referenced by Lave and Wenger.[33] The school as a place to group students for learning has a long history across different cultures, however, "schooling," such as universal primary education, is a relatively modern invention. It emphasizes structured learning with carefully designed curriculums and set goals and standards. In *Theory of Instruction*, Jerome Bruner stated that while theories of development and learning are descriptive, a theory of instruction "is prescriptive in the sense that it sets forth rules concerning the most effective way of achieving knowledge or skill."[34]

Linguistics

The acquisition of language, as discussed in human development theories, is dependent on cultural context, and therefore, linguistics is located at the edge between the "individual" and the "environment and culture" vertices of the triangle. Herbert Clark, in discussing the acquisition of deictic terms in early childhood, emphasizes the indispensable relationship between the development of language and the space we inhabit. According to Clark, what we perceive informs the semantics of our language.[35] Clark's theories on language and space is an important bridge to the design ideas explored in this book.

Map #3

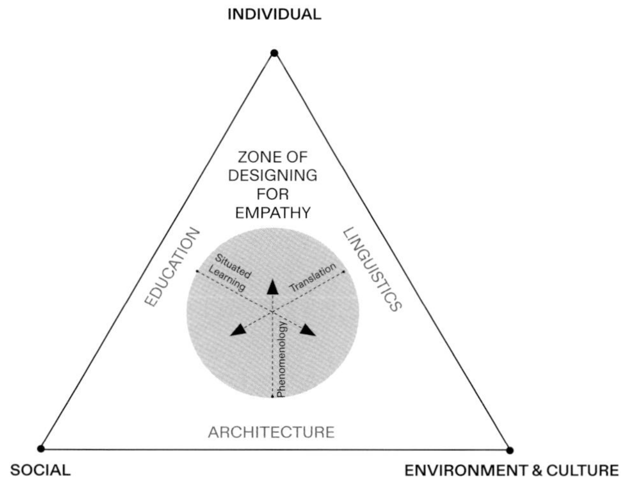

1.11 Map #3

The third map identifies how the disciplines of architecture, education, and linguistics interact with one another. The three forces that pull these disciplines from the edges to the center are "phenomenology" for architecture, "situated learning" for education, and "translations" for linguistics. Through phenomenology we can bring the focus of discussion in architecture to the experience of space; through situated learning the barriers of formal education dissolve and learning is contextualized; and through translations we learn other perspectives. At the convergence of these three disciplines lies what I call the "Zone of Designing for Empathy," from where the design conjectures proposed in this book emerged.

Phenomenology

The transformative power of architecture lies in how its concrete presence enables the creation of narratives—both visual and imaginative, engaging all sensory experiences that define profound impacts in people's lives. For instance, the smell of a school corridor, the window at the end of a hall, a lonely tree in the courtyard, or a bench that one sits on habitually, transcends

1.12 Le Corbusier. Notre-Dame du Haut, Ronchamp.

from their physical being into larger narratives in one's imagination. We can claim that all good architecture does that. Anyone who has set foot in Le Corbusier's Notre-Dame du Haut (1955) in Ronchamp can describe the narratives embedded in it, the spirituality that can be found, and the humanism that is shared by the same materials that define walls, doors, and roofs elsewhere but that fail to achieve this level of transcendence. It is this power to create a narrative of humanism that connects architecture with human development theories. This is particularly critical during early learning, a stage in development that profoundly impacts who we are and, by extension, what kind of a society we will become.

In his book *The Poetics of Space*, Gaston Bachelard proposes a systematic psychological study on analyzing the impact of intimate spaces in our lives, which he calls "topoanalysis."[36] Bachelard uses the house as the focus of his study and presents a topoanalytical line of questioning as follows: "Was the room a large one? Was the garret cluttered up? Was the nook warm? How was it lit? How, too, in these fragments of space, did the human being achieve silence? How did he relish the very special silence of the various retreats of solitary daydreaming?"[37] These questions are investigative of daydreaming, according to Bachelard, the primary benefit of the house. It is not a big stretch to reconstruct this line of topoanalytical questioning to understand the influence of the house in the cognitive development of early childhood, when dreams and reality are not separable.[38] In this type of phenomenological questioning lies a key bridge to understanding the relationship between the physical environment and human development.

Bachelard saw the house as the "the privileged entity for a phenomenological study."[39] I would argue that the only other architectural typology that has as strong an impact in our lives is the school. School is a place where a significant amount of time is spent during different stages of development. If we close our eyes, most of us can remember the first home we grew up in and the school we went to. Therefore, several case studies in this book focus on nursery through 12th grade schools, but the discussion expands to learning environments in a wider framework.

Situated Learning

According to Lave and Wenger, "Issues of learning and schooling seemed to have become too deeply interrelated in our culture...More importantly, the organization of schooling as an educational form is predicated on claims that knowledge can be decontextualized."[40] They highlight the contradiction in this decontextualization by pointing out that "schools themselves as social institutions and as places of learning constitute very specific contexts."[41] Advocates of place-based learning stress the importance of creating interpenetrations of the school into its context, fostering social, cultural, and environmental participations.

Situated learning as a link to the map's central Zone of Designing for Empathy indicates two key points as it relates to the design conjectures in this book. First, it is important to recognize that schools are not the exclusive realm of learning environments. Learning can and does happen in other social and cultural settings.[42] Therefore, the case studies include other building types such as museums, memorials, and installations. Secondly, the design conjectures showcase a deliberate effort to contextualize schools and to create constant interpenetrations with cultural and environmental contexts. These interpenetrations start even during the process of building the school. One such example is the Elementary School project in Marsassoum, Senegal, for which we designed a novel construction process that involves the participation of the community. As a result, building the school becomes a communal learning activity. (Figures 1.13–1.14) The development of creating a new construction system came from the knowledge that existing structures in Marsassoum, primarily built in clay bricks, didn't last more than five years, and that other construction systems frequently involve imported materials.

In our proposal, the primary materials for the school's construction are rammed earth, made up of local clay and sand, and locally sourced bamboo. Each step of the construction process is designed to eliminate waste. The rammed earth columns are created using a circular slip formwork strategy that enables them to be built without the need for elaborate scaffolding and formwork braces. The slip-forms can be reused multiple times, throughout the construction of the school, as well as for other local projects. To remove the need for scaffolding, the school's bamboo roof is built on the floor and then hoisted up to its final elevation. The project engages with the community by creating a new way of construction which will in turn allow them to build more structures and develop their local built environment.

In the Senegal Elementary School case study, the definition of the school "building" expands beyond being a place—defined with a noun—to becoming an act of building—defined with a verb. This conceptual shift of the school building from object to act situates learning deeply in the community.

1.13 Senegal Elementary School classroom pavilions are organized to form a central courtyard around the existing Moraceae tree.

1.14 (Following spread) Showing the construction sequencing for the school.

CIRCLING (the) EARTH

A TECTONIC STORY

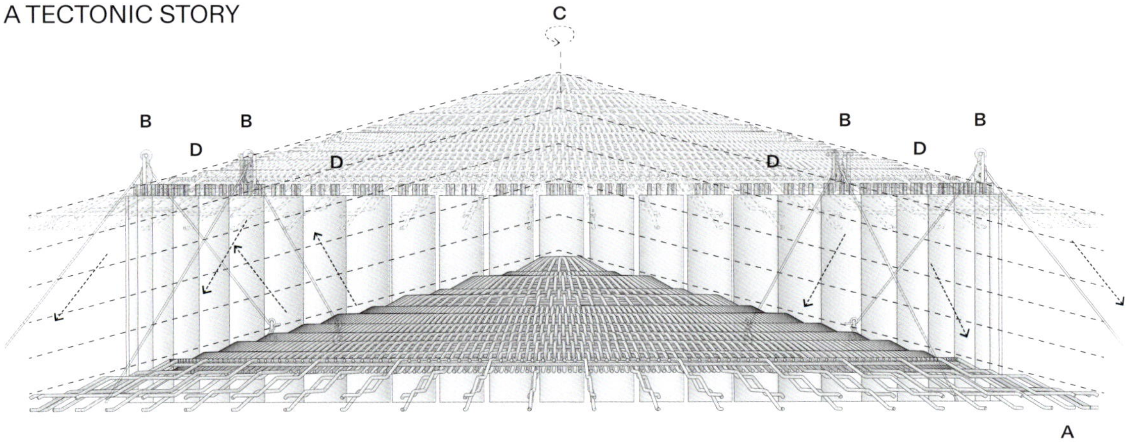

Woven bamboo roof construction:

The woven bamboo roof is built on the floor and then hoisted in place after completion. This method is used for ease of construction and to eliminate the need for scaffolding.

A Roof structure built at the ground
B Pulley and rope system to raise roof
C Roof rotation after hoisting (rotation angle: 280-mm radial segment)
D Bamboo roof members to weave into column reinforcement

1 A 600 mm diameter split PVC pipe will serve as the slip formwork. The formwork is lightweight and reusable.

2 Bamboo sticks are placed into the formwork as reinforcement. (6) 25 mm diameter sticks measuring a minimum of 700 mm long are needed for each pour.

3 The formwork is filled with compacted earth up to the rim of the formwork and it is rammed.

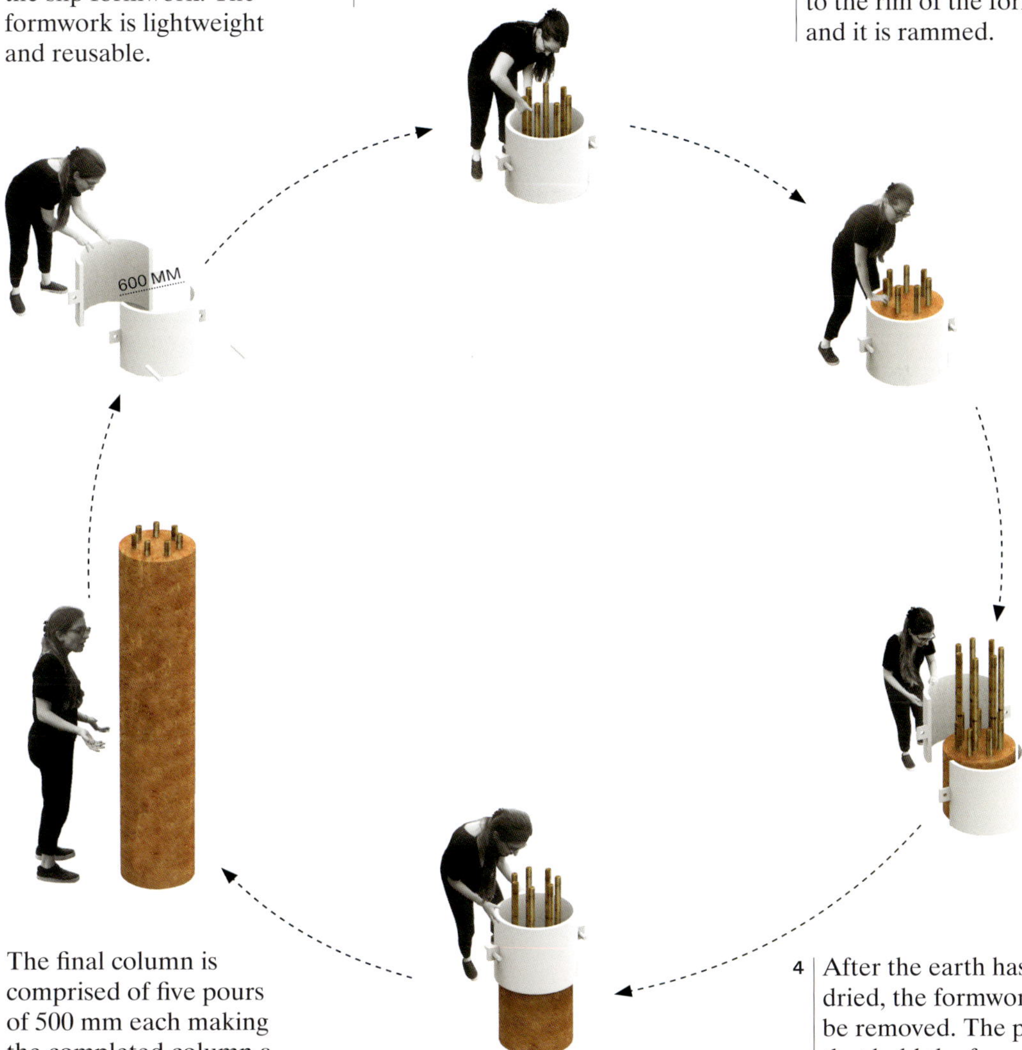

4 After the earth has dried, the formwork can be removed. The pins that hold the formwork are released and the two parts of the formwork are separated.

5 The formwork can now be moved up to create the next segment of the column. The same formwork can be used to create multiple pours.

6 The final column is comprised of five pours of 500 mm each making the completed column a total of 2.5 meters tall. The bamboo reinforcing should stick out from the top by 200 mm to allow for the roof connection.

Translations

Esra Akcan, in her seminal book *Translation in Architecture*, writes about a critical period of modern architectural history in Turkey as she "explores the concept of translation to explain interactions between places."[43] Akcan surveys theoretical frameworks of translation from the humanist perspectives of Octavio Paz and Walter Benjamin, and to Jacques Derrida's thesis of "untranslatability." She also warns us about the notions of translations in colonialism that can be used for cultural appropriation. Akcan's expansion of translation beyond language toward a broader spectrum includes "bi- and multilateral international transportation of people, ideas, technology, information and images."[44]

This extended understanding illustrates not only the potency of translation to enrich our experiences in myriad ways but also to help us leave ethnocentric points of views behind in an effort to move toward a more open and inclusive worldview. And Akcan reminds us, "Things do not get lost in translation, but they get multiplied through displacement and replacement."[45] It is in this recognition of the power of translation that Akcan's framework offers a critical shift from translation as a compromised state to one that is the necessary condition in the transformation of the broader cultural landscape and the creation of new cultural forms.

The importance of cultural translation, as brought to focus by Akcan, forms a critical link to the discussions on designing for empathy, where perspective taking, a key empathy development strategy, requires translation. In *The Cultural Nature of Human Development*, Barbara Rogoff writes, "Understanding one's own cultural heritage, as well as other cultural communities, requires taking the perspective of people of contrasting backgrounds."[46]

Now that we have decoded all the elements of the map, it is helpful to summarize what the central circle represents. At the convergence of multiple disciplines, the Zone of Designing for Empathy postulates that through the experience of purposefully constructed spaces in situated learning environments, we are nudged to take the perspective of the others. Therefore, the design conjectures in this book attempt to create spatial constructs that on one hand situate learning environments through interpenetrations with their context, and on the other hand, catalyze narratives that are generated through translations between different people, forms of life, ideas, emotions, images, languages, and cultures.

DESIGNING FOR EMPATHY CHAPTER NOTES

1 Juhani Pallasmaa, "Empathic and Embodied Imagination: Intuiting Experience and Life in Architecture," in *Architecture & Empathy* (Tapio Wirkkala-Rut Bryk Foundation, 2015), 5.

2 Karsten Stueber, "Empathy," in *Stanford Encyclopedia of Philosophy Archive*, Fall 2019, 3. https://plato.stanford.edu/archives/fall2019/entries/empathy/.

3 Robert K. Vischer, Harry Francis Mallgrave, and Eleftherios Ikonomou, *Empathy, Form, and Space: Problems in German Aesthetics, 1873–1893*, 1993, 21, http://ci.nii.ac.jp/ncid/BA22759272.

4 Vischer, Mallgrave, and Ikonomou, *Empathy, Form, and Space*, 92.

5 Vischer, Mallgrave, and Ikonomou, *Empathy, Form, and Space*, 97–98.

6 Vischer, Mallgrave, and Ikonomou, *Empathy, Form, and Space*, 29.

7 Christiane Montag, Jürgen Gallinat, and Andreas Heinz, "Theodor Lipps and the Concept of Empathy: 1851–1914," *American Journal of Psychiatry* 165, no. 10 (October 1, 2008): 1261, https://doi.org/10.1176/appi.ajp.2008.07081283.

8 Vernon Lee, *The Beautiful: An Introduction to Psychological Aesthetics* (Cambridge University Press, 1913); Edward Bradford Titchener, *A Text-Book of Psychology* (MacMillan, 1910).

9 Stueber, "Empathy," 3.

10 Christian Norberg-Schulz, *Genius Loci: Towards a Phenomenology of Architecture*, 1979, 5.

11 Stueber, "Empathy," 5.

12 Stueber, "Empathy," 19.

13 Stueber, "Empathy," 34.

14 Ilpo Koskinen, Katja Battarbee, and Tuuli Mattelmäki, *Empathic Design, User Experience in Product Design*, IT Press, 2003.

15 In discussing their projects for maternity wards in Tanzania and India, Sandman, Meguid, and Levänen distinguish different design processes depending on the distance between the designer and the user, and they argue that "Empathy can be one way to reduce distance and deepen the design process." They refer to Smeenk, Tomico, and van Turnhout's framework for "mixed perspectives" in empathic design, which helps identify the distance between designers and users in first-, second-, and third-person perspectives.

The conventional design process, during which the designer is entirely separated from the end user and their only connection is through the designer's empathic imagination, is understood as a third-person perspective. Whereas the second-person perspective is defined as "activating the users in collaborative exercises and therefore designing for a known other." It is considered a first-person perspective "when designers experienced the situation of the users personally, being part of the users' system."

Based on this, we can assign three subcategories of empathy in the design process to the mixed-perspectives framework as follows: empathic imagination is the third-person perspective; empathic design is the second-person perspective; and participatory/co-design is the first-person perspective.

For further reference, see: Helena Sandman, Tarek Meguid, and Jarkko Levänen, "Unboxing Empathy: Reflecting on Architectural Design for Maternal Health," *CoDesign* 18, no. 2 (October 26, 2020): 260–278, https://doi.org/10.1080/15710882.2020.1833935; Wina Smeenk, Oscar Tomico, and K.G. Van Turnhout, "A Systematic Analysis of Mixed Perspectives in Empathic Design: Not One Perspective Encompasses All," *International Journal of Design* 10, no. 2 (August 31, 2016): 31–48.

16 Pallasmaa, "Empathic and Embodied Imagination," 12.

17 Pallasmaa, "Empathic and Embodied Imagination," 12–13.

18 Excerpts from the letter written by the owner of Telluride House to Aybars Aşçı, February 2021. Printed with permission.

19 Cited by H.T. Cadbury-Brown, "Ludwig Mies van der Rohe," *AA Journal* 75, 834 (July–August 1959), 32.

20 Koskinen, Battarbee, and Mattelmäki, *Empathic Design, User Experience in Product Design*, 39–40.

21 Riccardo Manzotti, "Empathic Space and Shared Consciousness," in *Designing for Empathy: Perspectives on the Museum Experience*, ed. Elif M. Gökçiğdem (Rowman & Littlefield, 2019), 62–63.

22 Karl Popper, *Conjectures & Refutations* (Routledge, 2002), 60–61.

23 During the workshops for this book, Dr. Julia Higdon proposed other possible geometric representations for the mapping. Aşçı and Higdon agreed that the triangular mapping constructs the clearest representation for the purposes of this book.

24 William Crain, *Theories of Development* (Routledge, 2016), 241.

25 Crain, *Theories of Development*, 205.

26 Crain, *Theories of Development*, 217.

27 Barbara Rogoff, *The Cultural Nature of Human Development* (Oxford University Press, 2003), 3.

28 Rogoff, *The Cultural Nature of Human Development*, 11.

29 Helen Haste and Salie Abrahams, "Morality, Culture and the Dialogic Self: Taking Cultural Pluralism Seriously," *Journal of Moral Education* 37, no. 3 (September 1, 2008), 377–94.

30 Crain, *Theories of Development*, 248–49.

31 Urie Bronfenbrenner, *The Ecology of Human Development: Experiments by Nature and Design* (Harvard University Press, 1979).

32 "Lave and Wenger on Situated Learning - New Learning Online," n.d., https://newlearningonline.com/new-learning/chapter-6/supporting-material/lave-and-wenger-on-situated-learning.

33 Jean Lave and Étienne Wenger, *Situated Learning: Legitimate Peripheral Participation* (Cambridge University Press, 1991), 39.

34 Jerome S. Bruner, *Towards a Theory of Instruction* (The Belknap Press of Harvard University Press, 1966), 40.

35 Herbert Clark, "Space, time, semantics, and the child" in *Cognitive Development and the Acquisition of Language*, ed. T.E. Moore (Academic Press, 1973), 30.

36 Gaston Bachelard, *The Poetics of Space* (Penguin Books, 2014), 30.

37 Bachelard, *The Poetics of Space*, 31.

38 Jean Piaget, *The Child's Conception of the World* (Routledge & Kegan Paul Ltd., 1971), chapter III.

39 Bachelard, *The Poetics of Space*, 25.

40 Lave and Wenger, *Situated Learning: Legitimate Peripheral Participation*, 39–40.

41 Lave and Wenger, *Situated Learning*, 40.

42 For instance, in the apprenticeship model, Jean Lave gives the examples of tailor workshops in Liberia.

43 Akcan focuses on the relationship between Germany and Turkey during the period from approximately 1920–50, the early decades of the newly founded Turkish Republic. Esra Akcan, *Architecture in Translation*, Duke University Press, 2012, 3.

44 Akcan, *Architecture in Translation*, 3.

45 Akcan, *Architecture in Translation*, 26.

46 Rogoff, *The Cultural Nature of Human Development*, 11.

2

EMPATHY IN PERSPECTIVE

Dr. Julia Higdon

"Look again at that dot. That's here. That's home. That's us. On it everyone you love, everyone you know, everyone you ever heard of, every human being who ever was, lived out their lives. The aggregate of our joy and suffering, thousands of confident religions, ideologies, and economic doctrines, every hunter and forager, every hero and coward, every creator and destroyer of civilization, every king and peasant, every young couple in love, every mother and father, hopeful child, inventor and explorer, every teacher of morals, every corrupt politician, every 'superstar,' every 'supreme leader,' every saint and sinner in the history of our species lived there—on a mote of dust suspended in a sunbeam.

"The Earth is a very small stage in a vast cosmic arena. Think of the rivers of blood spilled by all those generals and emperors so that, in glory and triumph, they could become the momentary masters of a fraction of a dot. Think of the endless cruelties visited by the inhabitants of one corner of this pixel on the scarcely distinguishable inhabitants of some other corner, how frequent their misunderstandings, how eager they are to kill one another, how fervent their hatreds.

"Our posturings, our imagined self-importance, the delusion that we have some privileged position in the Universe, are challenged by this point of pale light. Our planet is a lonely speck in the great enveloping cosmic dark. In our obscurity, in all this vastness, there is no hint that help will come from elsewhere to save us from ourselves.

"The Earth is the only world known so far to harbor life. There is nowhere else, at least in the near future, to which our species could migrate. Visit, yes. Settle, not yet. Like it or not, for the moment the Earth is where we make our stand.

"It has been said that astronomy is a humbling and character-building experience. There is perhaps no better demonstration of the folly of human conceits than this distant image of our tiny world. To me, it underscores our responsibility to deal more kindly with one another, and to preserve and cherish the pale blue dot, the only home we've ever known."

— Carl Sagan, *Pale Blue Dot*, 1994

2.1 (Facing page) Planet Earth is visible as a bright speck within the sunbeam just right of center and appears softly blue.

THE IMPORTANCE AND MALLEABILITY OF EMPATHY

Empathy is feeling what others are feeling and understanding their situation. Empathy can inspire compassionate action at times or be conspicuously absent at times, and so there has been much debate about its value. While some researchers and theorists have promoted the virtues of empathy, others have urged us away from it, and others still have recognized empathy as a two-sided coin, with value and potential pitfalls.[1]

Researchers have shown that empathy helps improve intergroup relations, and there have been a plethora of interventions to enhance inclusion.[2] But there is a different case for empathy as well. Within individuals, the depth of understanding that leads to compassionate action comes from empathy. As we express throughout this book, we see empathy as a necessary motivating force that leads to deeper understanding. It supports a better comprehension of the world and wiser decision making. At the same time, we recognize limits and risks can come with emotionally charged and bias-laden territories. Most importantly, we argue that empathy is malleable and therefore can be guided. It can be promoted or suppressed. Thus, we see an opportunity where, with the design of space, empathy helps us stretch our perspective across long spans of time and wide distances, including those in our closest social networks, and those across continents and cultures, across species, and toward fragile ecosystems and the natural environment.

THE PROCESS OF EMPATHY

Empathy is not simply a state; it is a reaction and a process. The empathic reaction begins with a cue—perhaps we see someone in pain. The first reaction is a quick and emotional one. We feel the pain of others to some extent. Then the process of our own reflection, deepening understanding, evaluation, and decision making begins. We ask how they came to be in pain. We seek information that helps explain their pain or we remember a time when we were in a similar situation so we can understand what they might be dealing with through the analog of our own experience. We cognitively process the original cue, as well as the emotions that this raises, gather information, and come to a decision regarding how to act or what to do.

While there are countless variations and complications, this is generally how empathy unfolds.

When empathy is engaged, we have an approximate emotional sense, and we have an approximate cognitive understanding of what someone is feeling and experiencing. The emotional processes of empathy are apparent when we feel what others are feeling, not exactly but to a degree, giving us a deeper sense of what it is like to be in their shoes, in that moment. The cognitive side is apparent when we can surmise why they are in the situation that they're in, and we develop theories about how they arrived at this point and what their perspective about it might be. When it comes to both the emotional and cognitive processes of empathy, it's important to note that exact accuracy doesn't matter as much as plausibility.[3] These are theories and approximations because we aren't having the same experience ourselves. However, the closer we can come to approximate the experience of others, the more empathic and appropriate our reactions would be.

While we often focus on the role empathy plays in understanding the pain and suffering of others, it also applies to understanding their joys, contentment, and other states. Through empathy, we can more fully understand a wide range of experiences and internal states of others. Empathy leads to our ability to cooperate, because it is through empathy that we can appreciate goals that we have in common with others and be motivated to act to a wider benefit beyond our own.

The information we gain from feeling the emotions of others, and processing what we sense and know, helps lead to the fullest manifestation of empathy. The process of empathy draws heavily from perspective taking. In the opening passage, Carl Sagan asked us to zoom out. This is a unique perspective often provided by those who have looked on our Earth from a distance. This perspective reduces outsized views of our own importance. From the ground-level, some groups feel distant, and differences feel more pronounced. However, if we change our vantage point to that of distant onlookers, our similarities with these same groups become more pronounced. For many, this changed perspective is a moving experience that can provide understanding of important universals that we share.

This also highlights a primary position of this book, often overlooked in discussions of empathy, which is that we form our point of view from within a perspective that is not only internal and context-based, but also *spatial*. Not many developmental psychologists or social scientists have considered the geometry of empathy. The goal is therefore to merge human development theory with this spatial point of view. Very few humans have had the opportunity to view the Earth from afar and so this captivating perspective exists primarily in the imagination. The idea of this book is that shifting perspective in the immediate context and in the physical, spatial sense, enables shifting perspective in the cognitive and emotional senses.

HUMAN DEVELOPMENT THEORY

Before going further into how empathy develops, it is beneficial to spend some time on human development theory in general as the spatial theories build on this foundation. Theories of human development help explain patterns in the process of change over the course of human lives.[4] They can do three things in service of an exploration of empathy. First, they can describe observable milestones of development, such as the sequencing of increased cognitive abilities over time or the sequencing of social skills and participation in life within groups. These theories provide tools to understand what is most common at various approximate ages within a group through the observation of patterns of human behavior. They supply vocabulary to identify what a developmental period tends to include and what changes consistently happen over the lifespan.

Theories of human development also explain how and why these changes occur, when they are not directly observable. In this way, theories are concerned with explaining what influences this development, including biological processes, cultural norms, built and natural environments, routine everyday lived experiences, social groups and conditioning, and individual meaning-making. The study of human development provides several lenses through which we can explore the underlying processes that drive these major progressions—for example, the process of natural cognitive development, the exchanges between individuals and groups, the role of cultural contexts and environments—and how these forces influence patterns of change.

Finally, developmental theories help build an understanding of what enables individuals to develop, or to flourish, what puts individuals at risk, and what might serve as protections against these risks—the "so what" of these theories. In this way, human development theories help us pose well-reasoned hypotheses about the conditions that may influence, facilitate, or impede development. This is important to the discussion of empathy in this book, which poses several hypotheses on how purposeful design might lead us to a greater development of empathy. These are grounded in human development theory in general as well as theories of the development of empathy specifically.

These theories focus on major progressions in the knowledge, skills, or dispositions that humans come to possess over the lifespan, shifts that are durable for long periods versus temporary ebbs and flows, and shifts that can be observed as patterns among groups of people versus idiosyncratically among individuals. Similar to cultural psychologists Haste and Abrahams, in this book we define human development as increasing sophistication in the use of cultural tools to make meaning the world and gain expertise.[5] Further, three vantage points can be used to understand how empathy develops: within individuals, within their social groups, and within larger cultural contexts.

THE DEVELOPMENT OF EMPATHY WITHIN INDIVIDUALS

The first vantage point has to do with cognitive processes within an individual, or sensing and thinking, and their increasing sophistication. It centers around the subject as the individual, and patterns in how individuals incorporate new information and experiences into how they see the world.

Sensory processes are involved as some of the earliest building blocks of empathy in child development. Through sensing the internal states and experiences of others, we learn how to avoid or seek similar experiences ourselves.[6] As outlined by Piaget, infants experience the world through their senses, reflexes, and experimentation with the environment.[7] They attend what is readily available in their environment and build toward paying joint attention as pointing and gesturing become early forms of communication between infants and their caregivers.[8] As infants become more attuned to the expressions of their caregivers, and through observations of the pain of others, infants also feel a similar pain. As the capacity for memory develops, so does the ability to file that information away and then draw on it later.

In addition to the observations of infants sensing their environment and being attuned to their caregivers, Piaget also developed a comprehensive theory of the development of human cognition.[9] As an early researcher in intelligence testing, he observed patterns and similarities in the mistakes children made on these tests. Over the course of several decades, he built his seminal stage theory of human cognitive development that remains highly influential as of this writing. While the degree to which human development varies by culture led to new theories that take this into account, his original theories about how cognition develops, and our awareness of the milestone achievements that characterize this development, form the bedrock of our understanding of the development of empathy. Interestingly, because of the emphasis Piaget put on the skills of abstraction and language, as well as the development away from egocentrism to the inclusion of others as prerequisites for the development of empathy, he didn't believe empathy was possible until children were much older, at least age seven. Since Piaget's time, researchers have explored in more detail the sensory and emotional inputs involved in early human development through the development of the Theory of Mind.

Theory of Mind describes the ability to infer another person's mental state, such as their emotions, beliefs, and motivations. It's a theory because we cannot directly observe another person's mental state, and it's directed toward understanding what's going on in their mind.[10] Critically, it involves an understanding that the internal mental states of others differ from one's own, which is an understanding that increases in early childhood. This developmental ability has been observed in children younger than two years as well as in research involving children around the age of four.[11] Further, the ability to differentiate oneself from others is a crucial skill in the development of empathy that has its roots in Theory of Mind.[12] This is important to help deal with a difficult challenge of empathy, which is to feel another person's pain without suffering so much that we can't effectively take compassionate action.

While the general process of empathy is consistent, we differ as individuals in our capacity for empathy. Some individuals feel the emotions of others more strongly, some cognitively process information more quickly and efficiently, and individual empathy differs in other ways as well. Genetics and personality account for some of these differences. Just like intelligence, genetics partly determines our empathic ability because empathy involves cognitive ability. The extent of understanding how someone else is feeling, or our ability to take their perspective, is supported by cognitive ability. Genetics and biology, as well as many other social and environmental factors, such as access to resources and experiences, wealth, marginalization, and stress influence the development of sophisticated empathic processes. The processes involved in the development of empathy that can be attributable to lived experiences are more relevant to how we can foster empathy in the environments that are the focus of this book.

Our ability to plausibly approximate how another being is feeling or what they're experiencing increases with age, as we practice the skills of perspective taking and receive feedback through our experiences and interactions.[13] Empathy develops within individuals over our lifespans as our outlook and responses to others change over time. We gain increasing sensory and cognitive skills, expand the tools that we have available to make meaning of experience, and gain wisdom as we age. In our everyday, routine experiences, our outlooks and reactions are gradually shaped, and in the earliest stages this gradual shaping is without our awareness or direct reflection. We have experiences with larger impact, that may shift our outlook and alter our future actions in more dramatic steps. In these cases, it is not merely the experience, but the reflection on these experiences, that causes changes to empathy and future empathic actions, and this is what differentiates these transformational experiences from those that are more routine.

THE DEVELOPMENT OF EMPATHY WITHIN SOCIAL GROUPS

The second vantage point regarding how empathy develops has to do with social processes and social interactions. Vygotsky was one of the first psychologists to challenge the dominant cognitive theory of Piaget. In this line of thinking, development is an individual change process within a physical setting and social environment. According to Social Learning Theory, we learn the most when we work with more experienced and more capable others, specifically those who are at a level that is more advanced than ourselves but that is achievable with some inspiration and support. Social interaction allows the use of tools and ways of thinking that would not be possible otherwise, and it is in that "Zone of Proximal Development" that development occurs.[14] In this book, we suggest that the zone is not just social but also physical, and as such can also viewed as the space in which proximal development takes place.

Social groups also operate in some ways like an apprenticeship. According to Lave and Wenger, communities of practice are groups that have regular interaction with a purpose in common, such as an apprenticeship in a profession or a classroom within a school, in which there is a specific domain of interest and learning is a part of a social practice.[15] Experience is extended over time and there is a shared commitment to the specific goals of the community.[16] In these communities of practice, individuals participate on the periphery at first, and then move toward full participation as the goal. Through increasingly central participation, learners negotiate meaning from complex social practices.[17] Most importantly, communities of practice involve doing, and "[it] is doing in a historical and social context that gives structure and meaning to what we do."[18] Regular, warm interactions also may increase social networks in which social norms are practiced and shared.[19] From this perspective, development is a participatory change process of observation and engagement with the activities of various social communities.

There is an element of physical space involved with the Zone of Proximal Development and communities of practice that is not often discussed when theorizing about the supports we receive to learn. Taking the Zone of Proximal Development literally, at the youngest ages, when empathy first develops, the Zone of Proximal Development is best reflected in closer proximity, and possibly the most desirable scale of the physical space is smaller. At a very young age, most interactions happen within dyads: a parent and a child, a teacher and a child, a peer and a child. And many smaller spaces, such as kitchen tables or small nooks in a playground, reflect a closeness that is inherent in dyads. It is through close interaction, at this stage, that the sensory perception discussed earlier becomes possible. As humans develop and more context is available to our perception and larger groups become part of our experience, networks move from dyads to small groups and then larger groups. Similarly, a wider Zone of Proximal Development becomes available, and spaces are more varied in scale and design. We can begin to experiment with more variety in perspective taking, and spatial perspectives can similarly include more points of view and intentional shifts to different views. In this way, the architectural examples in this book reflect a sensitivity to the Zone of Proximal Development and can guide us to consider the development of empathy in new ways from within a spatial realm.

THE DEVELOPMENT OF EMPATHY WITHIN CULTURAL CONTEXTS

It is important to note that development involves working with a more experienced other to use the tools found within the culture. A major advance in Vygotsky's theorizing was understanding that literacy is a cultural tool that facilitates the development of cognitive skills.[20] This development later helped explain cross-cultural variation in the manifestation of skills and why developmental stages stopped making sense when applied outside of industrialized Western societies.[21] This brings us to the third vantage point regarding how empathy develops: cultural context. This vein of human development theory has grown as theorists have explored how patterns in human development are substantially different in different cultural contexts.

The importance of examining culture and environment was also highlighted by Vygotsky, who postulated that the individual must be understood within the context of social-historical processes, institutions, and activities in which the individual is a part; as well as Bronfenbrenner who proposed an ecological system to understand the individual in their context.[22] These models diagrammed or mapped the variety of influences upon individuals, depicting some farther away and some closer to an individual.

However, it is most helpful to think of development within contexts as forming a developmental niche. According to Super and Harkness, this niche includes the details of the environment and mapping developmental niches "makes available to scientific scrutiny the process by which culture affects the course of development."[23] Their theory helps us understand and specify the relevant processes that impact how humans develop within niches that are unique to them and include individual cognition and processing, parenting and intimate social groups, and larger cultural processes. In order to learn, we participate within our developmental niche. This expansion of theory included the ways in which types and levels of participation vary by culture.[24]

The developmental perspective of Haste and Abrahams is especially helpful because it outlines how individuals make meaning and generate individual and societal change from within their social groups through an increasing sophistication of the use of tools such as language, myths, and narratives that are available within their culture.[25] The process of culture and the use of cultural tools are important ways in which individuals make meaning of events and situations that evoke empathy, evaluate what others might be thinking or feeling, identify legitimate or acceptable actions, and make decisions about what to do. When we focus on culture as a process, it shifts our thinking away from culture as a monolithic scaffold or structure within which we operate and that constrains our actions, toward culture as including a dynamic system of shared values and beliefs that are transmitted, processed, utilized, and changed by members of that culture. A primary way that this process takes place is through the language, stories, myths, and legends of that culture.[26] These are the tools that we use to make meaning of our experiences and that guide our individual thinking, as well as how we act and react within groups and with members of other groups. They are also the tools that we use to communicate and transmit this meaning to others. It is through our dialogues and discussions that these worldviews are both invoked and changed over time.

When we use the stories and metaphors available within a culture, we are recalling and drawing from a variety of societal worldviews and principles that enable us to make meaning of experiences and decide how to act and what to do. This is the pluralism of a variety of approaches to situations that invoke empathy across different cultures, with advanced thinkers within a culture making sophisticated use of cultural tools to come to decisions. And while it is true that, within a given culture, certain principles are more dominant than others, individuals within a culture have a wide variety of these tools that are accessible to call upon to make meaning and make decisions. We have access to a coexistent multiplicity of voices through the examples of great novels or poetry, not just a single voice, which Bakhtin conceptualized as polyphony.[27] The process of human development is a process by which our selection and use of these cultural tools becomes more sophisticated and integrated over a lifespan or over generations, and not merely the advancement of individual cognitive and social ability. Experts gain a mastery of a wide variety of these cultural tools, and this is what enables complex reasoning and wise decision making within their context. Human development is the progression toward this expertise.

Cultural groups share a variety of ethical and moral standards. These standards define who is deserving of empathy, why, and what the range of acceptable responses to a given situation would be. Within larger cultural groups, members have access to a variety of tools available to communicate these standards and to make sense of experience. We also have opportunities to observe, practice, and reflect on examples of empathy from within social groups. Practice hones the development of individual empathic skills and decision making within the cultural context of the group.

In summary, empathy develops within individuals through participation in social groups and using cultural tools. As humans gain increasing sophistication in sensory and cognitive ability over time, empathy grows through increased ability to feel what others are feeling, understand an increasingly complex system of possible causes, and determine effective strategies to act when needed. Through working with more sophisticated others in social groups that start with the parent-child relationship and expand to larger groups and groups for distinct purposes as we age, we observe and participate in social interactions that demand empathy, and we stretch our range of understanding and the effectiveness of our responses to others. Through these groups and social interactions, we make increasingly sophisticated use of a wider variety of cultural tools to define the imperatives that are relevant in a situation, create paradigms of inclusion regarding who deserves empathy and why, and influence the culture through our participation and behaviors within this larger context. In this view, learning to be empathic is a process of development and of practice, where we develop our ability with other people and with increased sophistication in using and shaping the tools of the cultural contexts we inhabit.

EMPATHY CAN BE LIMITED OR SUPPRESSED

Up to this point, the goal of this discussion has been to shed light on how empathy develops. But we're not always empathic, and we don't always make empathic decisions. Biases and the way social groups are formed, perceive threat, and compete lead to us-versus-them thinking and behavior, where we're empathic toward "us" and not empathic toward "them."

Because thinking requires energy, we take cognitive shortcuts in order to engage in everyday life. Reading is an illustrative example. We do not observe every letter in words or even read every word in a sentence or paragraph when we read. If we did, reading would be laborious and exhausting. Instead, we only focus on key parts of words and keywords in a sentence when we read to pick up the pace. We fill in the rest through recognition of pattern and imagery. These shortcuts allow us to function in an information-rich, highly stimulating world.

Cognitive biases are best described as identifiable patterns in thinking that lead to major errors in understanding and bad decision-making. These are flaws in our thinking that are predictable and cause problems. And these patterns in thinking lead to patterns in behavior that reinforce the thinking. There are a great many biases that have been identified and described by scientists, however, the bias most relevant to a discussion on empathy is in-group/out-group bias.

We form groups with whom we cooperate—in-groups—and this process also defines groups of others—out-groups—who are not in our group and with whom we don't cooperate. In other words, "humans were designed for cooperation, but only with some people," according to Joshua Greene.[28] This bias shows up in a variety of ways. We're more likely to believe and trust members of our in-group than out-groups, more likely to cooperate with members of our in-group and to compete with members of out-groups, and more likely to favor policies and systems that suppress out-groups. This bias draws a boundary around who we consider worthy of our empathy, while excluding others. As our affinity for our in-group grows, so does our malice and unkindness toward out-groups.[29]

Social Identity Theory (SIT) helps explain the ways in which seeing ourselves as a member of a group develops, and how the categories we apply to ourselves and to others motivate our decisions. Individuals derive their social identity from their group memberships and identify themselves with multiple specific groups. SIT also defines a specific in-group along the lines of shared political, economic, and cultural resources; and defines the relevant out-groups as those who are competitors to these resources.[30]

Self-Categorization Theory (SCT) describes the process of categorization required to define who we are and who others are as groups and offers an explanation of when we shift from interpersonal to intergroup norms and behavior.[31] Turner and Oakes describe this shift as, "the effect of self-perception becoming more social categorical under certain conditions: group behavior is simply individuals acting in terms of a shared social identity."[32] By subsuming, under certain conditions, individual identity within a social category, identity is depersonalized. The self is seen as somewhat, but not completely, interchangeable with other representatives of the same category because relevant characteristics are shared at the categorical level. Self-categorization depends on personal identification with the perceived distinctiveness of the group, in comparison to other groups, as well as the adoption of the prevailing norms of the group.[33]

An illustrative example is national identity. SCT represents a level of social identity that is more abstract, however, this has to do with levels of inclusiveness and exclusiveness rather than being more versus less real. For example, given the prevalence of national discourses, the salience of national norms, and the direct impact of laws and institutions, national identity is highly relevant for many individuals. Historically, the identification of the national in-group as politically sovereign, along with the right to self-determination, was the basis of the nation-state. According to Habermas, the nation was originally a community of ethnic and linguistic descent, which, over time, was replaced by a definition along national and citizenship lines. Citizenship became pragmatic, as a safeguard of rights, adding functions and protections to national identification.[34] By way of example, this is how national identity can define who is entitled to empathy and who is not, based on group beliefs regarding rights to shared resources.

However, social identities and categories can be far less complex than national identity and can even be temporary. In experimental studies, Tajfel and colleagues found that categorization, even without a substantive basis for category membership, can be a sufficient condition to discriminate against the out-group, referred to as the minimal group paradigm.[35] In their studies, participants were grouped in meaningless ways, and were later asked to allocate monetary reward to others, not themselves. Contrary to expectation, subjects distributed the funds either fairly, or by discriminating systematically based on group membership, and not randomly given lack of relevant information about the recipients. Indeed, one identifiable strategy that the subjects seemed to employ was that which "maximizes difference" between groups, such that out-groups specifically receive less rewards, even at the expense of absolute in-group reward.

However, social categorization is often brought into sharper focus, and the effects augmented, by a perception of threat.[36] According to Realistic Group-Conflict Theory (RCT), a conflict of interest—for example competition over scarce goods—leads to group conflict.[37] This conflict forms the basis for self-identification with a dominant group that has the power to secure scarce resources. Thus, while categorization may be sufficient to prompt in-group favoritism and sometimes out-group discrimination, when social categories and identities are also combined with real or perceived competition or threat, empathy toward outgroup members becomes even harder to attain. This is also illustrated through the "Robbers Cave" field experiment conducted by Sherif and colleagues in the 1950s.[38] Researchers randomly divided adolescent boys in a summer camp into two groups. In the first phase of the study in-group identification was developed through cooperation within the group and without knowledge of the other group. In the second phase of the study, the existence of the other group was introduced as well as competition between the groups, thus forming an in-group and an out-group. Predictably, according to this theory, group friction and later conflict ensued during the second phase of the study. These conflicts persisted during attempts to reconcile in the third phase of the study, except when the boys pursued goals requiring cooperation between the groups.

Cultural and social ideologies, and myths that narrate them, also work to entrench in-group and out-group threat and competition. Social Dominance

Theory posits that all human societies have social hierarchies in place, grounded in ideologies that enhance the superiority of one group over others.[39] These are myths that legitimize hierarchy, such as anti-Black racism, Social Darwinism, and meritocracy. Institutions and policies based in these myths tend to maintain oppressive hierarchies. Social Dominance Orientation represents the degree to which an individual desires the domination of groups considered to be inferior and the degree to which the individual in question endorses myths that legitimize this. These are forces that weaken empathy to members of out-groups through exclusion and strengthen empathy to members of in-groups through inclusion.

We can see how these complex dynamics shape the development of empathy, and either the expression or curtailment of empathy, with a quote from a teacher of language and literature in the Czech Republic:

> A typical example is the Roma question. Students say that of course they do not mind skin colour and that we do not need to talk about it. I try to explain that the Roma have a different culture and that we can mutually enrich each other, but the discussion usually goes in the direction of criminality issues or the misuse of social benefits.[40]

In this example, the in-group being invoked is the national in-group, which has the power to provide resources such as security and social benefits. The students identify an out-group, the Roma, in the way they perceive the group as a threat and in competition for these resources. Skin color is described as unnecessary to talk about, however, it forms the basis of the categorization of the out-group that is seen as a threat. It is the combination of bias, social identification and categorization, social hierarchies, and threat, that leads to discrimination in the wider society. This combination draws a boundary between groups who are believed to be deserving of empathy, versus those that are not.

EMPATHY CAN BE FOSTERED THROUGH DESIGN

As complex and dynamic as these processes are, it is our position that empathy is malleable. It can be elevated, and its suppression can be counteracted.

The goal of this chapter has been to explore the development of empathy, and some of the major forces that push and pull us toward greater or lesser empathy. These connections highlight possibilities where intentional design can support the development of empathy.

The cognitive biases and errors in thinking described above are worsened by cognitive load. It takes a great deal of work to counteract forces that define categories and in-groups and out-groups. An idea presented in this book is that thoughtful design can lessen the cognitive load that it takes to take a different point of view. There are possibilities here in the planning of space and intentionally shifting positions within space, and in changing someone's viewpoint geometrically toward meaningful objects and people. Continued experiences like this may make it easier to be less egocentric and less protective, and help make taking multiple perspectives more common, natural, and inspirational.

Remaining in default mode also increases our tendency toward bias. Many of our reactions to the world around us are more automatic and less deliberate. For the most part, we automatically take certain routes and engage in routine actions. Another way in which the design of space can counteract this is by disrupting routine patterns, for example by piquing interest, sparking curiosity, or destabilizing states of equilibrium. Curiosity itself is a driving force behind being interested in recognizing and responding to novel environments and experiences, especially deepening our understanding of others who are very different from ourselves in space or time.

Enhanced environments can augment natural human development. This is particularly true in places where children spend a great deal of time, such as at home or at school. In early childhood, enhanced environments include opportunities for children to play, to experience their world through moving their bodies, and to explore a wide range of resources around them. Driven by their interest, and through the visceral experiences of their environment, children develop skills of sensing and perception, which are important in empathy. Social interactions can be fostered and expanded within the environment as well. When children are very young, the most important form of social interaction is in a dyad and social development takes place in very close proximity. As children get older, social interactions become more varied as children participate in larger social groups. Enhanced environments can facilitate both proximity and wider, more varied participation with others that help deepen empathy.

Empathy can be guided through curated perspective taking. Perspective taking is a crucial skill in the development of empathy, however, efforts to build this skill can overemphasize intellectual exercises or discussion-based practices. In the example from the classroom discussing the Roma cultural group, coaching students in taking multiple perspectives might include challenging the students to view the world from the point of view of a representative of this group. While helpful, this is a thought experiment. Barriers that run along national, cultural, or economic lines are difficult to counteract.

Within the design of space, thought experiments can be transformed into concrete experiences. An illustrative example that is discussed in this book is a design of a structure surrounding a piece of the Berlin Wall that is recontextualized in a public park in Lower Manhattan. The design created juxtapositions of different cultural contexts and times to allow a new narrative to emerge, one that brings us questions about humanism in the era of emerging nationalism and celebration of border walls. In this example, the guided perspective taking is dramatic and moving. We hypothesize that experiences like this might help deepen understanding and facilitate the development of empathy.

This book makes a unique contribution by promoting perspective taking literally, as a spatial construct. Creating opportunities to experience different perspectives through the design of the physical environment has the potential to promote the skills of empathy naturally and viscerally, potentially making the experience more transformative for the individuals in these spaces. The art of architectural design may also help shift perspectives toward universals rather than particulars, and to shift us out of default modes of thinking. The elevation of the perspective we take can make a difference in whether we see others as competitors and threats, or as fellow humans inhabiting an ecosystem contained within a pale, blue dot.

EMPATHY IN PERSPECTIVE
CHAPTER NOTES

1 Roman Krznaric, *Empathy: Why It Matters, and How to Get It* (Penguin, 2014); Paul Bloom, *Against Empathy: The Case for Rational Compassion* (Ecco, 2016); Elizabeth N. Simas, Scott Clifford, and Justin H. Kirkland, "How Empathic Concern Fuels Political Polarization," *American Political Science Review* 114, no. 1 (October 31, 2019): 258–69; Robert M. Sapolsky, *Behave: The Biology of Humans at Our Best and Worst* (Penguin, 2017); Işıl Çelimli and Julia Higdon, "Putting Writing into Perspective: Cultivating Empathy through High-Intensity Writing Practice," *Journal of Educational Research* 112, no. 6 (November 2, 2019): 710–20.

2 John F. Dovidio et al., "Empathy and Intergroup Relations." *American Psychological Association EBooks*, 2010, 393–408; Krystina A. Finlay and Walter G. Stephan, "Improving Intergroup Relations: The Effects of Empathy on Racial Attitudes," *Journal of Applied Social Psychology* 30, no. 8 (2000): 1720–37; For a review of interventions aimed toward children, see: Frances E. Aboud et al., "Interventions to Reduce Prejudice and Enhance Inclusion and Respect for Ethnic Differences in Early Childhood: A Systematic Review," *Developmental Review* 32, no. 4 (December 1, 2012): 307–36.

3 Silvia Diazgranados, Robert L. Selman, and Michelle Dionne, "Acts of Social Perspective Taking: A Functional Construct and the Validation of a Performance Measure for Early Adolescents," *Social Development* 25, no. 3 (October 2, 2015): 572–601.

4 Barbara M. Newman and Philip R. Newman, *Theories of Human Development* (Psychology Press, 2015).

5 Helen Haste and Salie Abrahams, "Morality, Culture and the Dialogic Self: Taking Cultural Pluralism Seriously," *Journal of Moral Education* 37, no. 3 (September 1, 2008): 377–94.

6 Sapolsky, *Behave: The Biology of Humans at Our Best and Worst.*

7 Jean Piaget, *Language and Thought of the Child: Selected Works* Vol 5, 2013.

8 Simon Baron-Cohen, "Precursors to a theory of mind: Understanding attention in others." *Natural theories of mind: Evolution, development and simulation of everyday mindreading* 1 (1991): 233–251.

9 Carol Garhart Mooney, *Theories of Childhood, Second Edition: An Introduction to Dewey, Montessori, Erikson, Piaget & Vygotsky* (Redleaf Press, 2013).

10 David Premack and Guy Woodruff, "Does the Chimpanzee Have a Theory of Mind?," *Behavioral and Brain Sciences* 1, no. 4 (December 1, 1978): 515–26.

11 Ronit Roth-Hanania, Maayan Davidov, and Carolyn Zahn-Waxler, "Empathy Development from 8 to 16 Months: Early Signs of Concern for Others," *Infant Behavior & Development* 34, no. 3 (June 1, 2011): 447–58; Jean Decety, "The Neurodevelopment of Empathy in Humans," *Developmental Neuroscience* 32, no. 4 (January 1, 2010): 257–67.

12 Nancy Eisenberg and Richard A. Fabes, "Empathy: Conceptualization, Measurement, and Relation to Prosocial Behavior," *Motivation and Emotion* 14, no. 2 (June 1, 1990): 131–49.

13 Çelimli and Higdon, "Putting Writing into Perspective: Cultivating Empathy through High-Intensity Writing Practice."

14 L.S. Vygotsky, *Mind in Society: The Development of Higher Psychological Processes* (Harvard University Press, 1980); L.S. Vygotsky, *The Collected Works of L. S. Vygotsky: Problems of General Psychology, Including the Volume Thinking and Speech* (Springer, 2011).

15 Jean Lave and Étienne Wenger, "Legitimate peripheral participation in communities of practice," *Distributed Learning*, Mary Lea and Kathy Nicholl, eds. (Routledge, 2002): 56–63.

16 Penelope Eckert, "Communities of Practice," *Encyclopedia of Language and Linguistics*, 2nd Edition, Keith Brown, ed. (Elsevier, 2006): 683–85.

17 Gill Kirkup, "11 Identity, community and distributed learning," *Distributed Learning: Social and cultural approaches to practice* (Routledge, 2013): 152.

18 Étienne Wenger, *Communities of Practice: Learning, Meaning, and Identity* (Cambridge University Press, 1999).

19 Robert D. Putnam, *Bowling Alone: The Collapse and Revival of American Community* (Simon and Schuster, 2000).

20 Vygotsky, *Mind in Society: The Development of Higher Psychological Processes*.

21 Barbara Rogoff, *The Cultural Nature of Human Development* (Oxford University Press, 2003).

22 Vygotsky, *Mind in Society: The Development of Higher Psychological Processes;* Urie Bronfenbrenner, *The Ecology of Human Development: Experiments by Nature and Design* (Harvard University Press, 1979).

23 Charles M. Super and Sara Harkness, "The Developmental Niche: A Conceptualization at the Interface of Child and Culture," *International Journal of Behavioral Development* 9, no. 4 (December 1, 1986): 545–69; and Charles M. Super and Sara Harkness, "Culture Structures the Environment for Development," *Human Dcvclopment* 45, no. 4 (January 1, 2002): 271.

24 Super and Harkness, "Culture Structures the Environment for Development."

25 Haste and Abrahams, "Morality, Culture and the Dialogic Self: Taking Cultural Pluralism Seriously."

26 Haste and Abrahams, "Morality, Culture and the Dialogic Self: Taking Cultural Pluralism Seriously."

27 Mikhail Bakhtin, " Dostoevsky's Polyphonic Novel and Its Treatment in Critical Literature," *Problems of Dostoevsky's Poetics* 8 (1984): 5–46.

28 Joshua David Greene, *Moral Tribes: Emotion, Reason, and the Gap Between Us and Them* (Penguin Press HC, 2013).

29 Sapolsky, *Behave: The Biology of Humans at Our Best and Worst*; see also Robert Sapolsky, "This Is Your Brain on Nationalism," *Foreign Affairs* 98, no. 2 (2019): 42–47.

30 Rupert Brown, *Prejudice: Its Social Psychology* (Wiley-Blackwell, 2010).

31 Henri Tajfel and John C. Turner, "An Integrative Theory of Intergroup Conflict," *Rediscovering Social Identity*, T. Postmes and N. R. Branscombe, eds. (2010): 173–90.

32 John Turner and Katherine J. Reynolds, "Self-Categorization Theory," *SAGE Publications* Ltd EBooks, 2012, 399–417.

33 Stephen D. Reicher, Russell Spears, and Tom Postmes, "A social identity model of deindividuation phenomena," *European Review of Social Psychology* 6, no. 1 (1995): 161–98.

34 Jürgen Habermas, *Between Facts and Norms: Contributions to a Discourse Theory of Law and Democracy* (Mit Press, 1998).

35 Henri Tajfel, "Experiments in Intergroup Discrimination," *Scientific American* 223, no. 5 (1970): 96–103.

36 Marilynn B. Brewer, "The Importance of Being We: Human Nature and Intergroup Relations," American Psychologist 62, no. 8 (January 1, 2007): 728–38.

37 Henri Tajfel and John C. Turner, "An Integrative Theory of Intergroup Conflict."

38 Sherif Muzafer and University of Oklahoma Intergroup Relations Project, *Experimental Study of Positive and Negative Intergroup Attitudes between Experimentally Produced Groups: Robbers Cave Study*, 1954.

39 Felicia Pratto et al., "Social Dominance Orientation: A Personality Variable Predicting Social and Political Attitudes," *Journal of Personality and Social Psychology* 67, no. 4 (October 1, 1994): 741–63.

40 Dana Moree, Cees Klaassen, and Wiel Veugelers, "Teachers' ideas about multicultural education in a changing society: the case of the Czech Republic." *European Educational Research Journal* 7, no. 1 (2008): 60–73.

3

DEIXIS AND EMPATHY

Learning to take perspectives

Before we learn how to speak, we communicate with deictic expressions. For instance, when a toddler points to an object with their finger, they are talking to us, by using their body language. They want us to pick up that object and bring it to them. Since the use of deictic expressions precedes our language acquisition, we subsequently experience a process of translation from using our bodies to the semantics of language. This process of translation continues in later stages of human development, when it expands from deictic expressions to spatial cognition—our ability to connect with our physical and social environment.

"Deixis, from the Greek verb meaning 'to point,' refers to words and to non-verbal features of communication like nods and gestures, which serve to point to or in some way to identify people, times, places and objects in the course of discourse."[1]

Deictic words and phrases are typically categorized in space, time, and person.[2] For instance [here] and [there], or [this] and [that] are considered "spatial" deictic words. They are dependent on the speaker's location in space. An object referred to as [here] can become [there] if the speaker's position changes vis-à-vis the object. Spatial deictics also exist in non-verbal expressions such as pointing with a finger to a near or further location, signifying a proximal or non-proximal condition.

On the other hand, temporal or time deixis is dependent on the point in time when the speaker talks, or when the utterance takes place in relation to the present moment. For instance, [tomorrow] will become [today], as time moves on. [Now] refers to the temporary existence of the moment, and an expression like [soon], which is conditioned to [now], is highly variable in

3.1 (Facing page) Avenues Silicon Valley Student Commons.

the specifics of the sociocultural context. For instance, [soon] in a leisurely setting, as in "I will see you soon," versus in a transportation hub, as in "Your plane will board soon," can mean vastly different amounts of time.

Personal deixis is the grammatical person in the utterance, linguistically defined as the speaker or the first person, while the addressee is the second person, and others in presence or the people who are referenced are the third person.[3]

Charles Fillmore, in his lectures on deixis at the University of California, adds two more categories: discourse deixis and social deixis.[4] He defines discourse deixis as "the matrix of linguistic material within which the utterance has a role, that is, the preceding and following parts of the discourse."[5] As an example, in the following sentence, [this] is discourse deictic:

> I met a colleague of yours last weekend. Well, [this] person told me some funny stories about your office.

Fillmore's second additional category is social deixis which he refers to as "The social relationships on the part of the participants in the conversation, that determine, for example, the choice of honorific or polite or intimate or insulting speech levels."[6]

DEICTIC CENTER

Deictic words and expressions are anchored to a specific point that constitutes the "deictic center." Stephen Levinson describes these specific points, each corresponding to a person, space, time, discourse, and social center, as such:

> (i) the central person is the speaker, (ii) the central time is the time at which the speaker produces the utterance, (iii) the central place is the speaker's location at utterance time or CT, (iv) the discourse center is the point which the speaker is currently at in the production of his utterance, and (v) the social center is the speaker's social status and rank, to which the status of rank of addressees or referents is relative.[7]

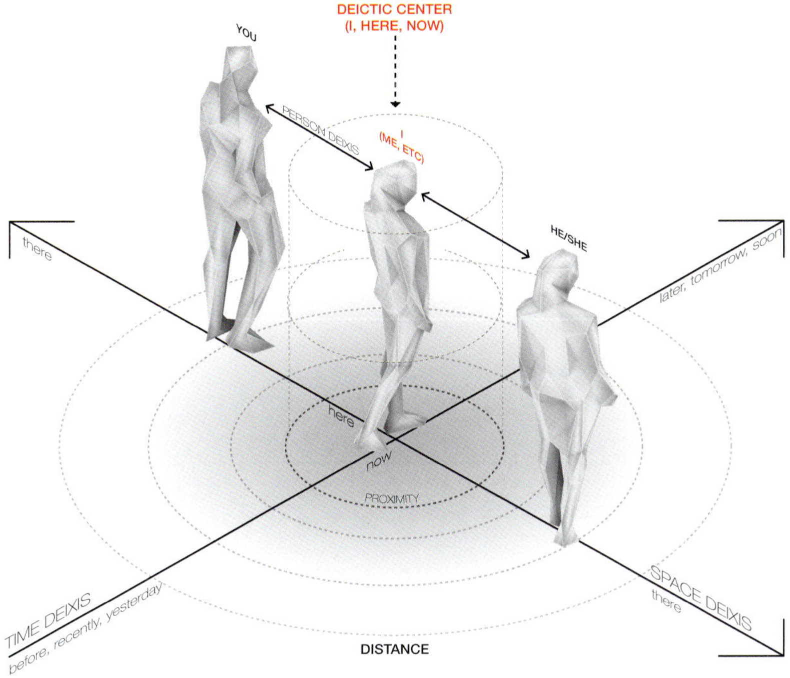

3.2 Deictic center. The diagram is based on Stephen Levinson's description.

In all the points listed above, the deictic expressions are indexed to the speaker, who is located at the center of this construct. Levinson explains the geometric construct of the deictic center as a four-dimensional space,

> composed of the three dimensions of space plus that of time, in which a speaker stands at the center. Radiating out from the speaker are a number of concentric circles distinguishing different zones of spatial proximity; through the speaker passes a 'time line', on which events prior to his present utterance, and events prior to those, can be linearly arranged, and similarly events at points and spans in the future; while the discourse to which the speaker contributes unfolds along this same time line. To capture the social aspects of deixis, we would need to add at least one further dimension, say of relative rank, in which the speaker is socially higher, lower or equal to the addressee and other persons that might be referred to.[8]

As illustrated in Figure 3.2, the deictic center has a clear focal point to which the deictic expressions relate. This creates an egocentric construct for the speaker, who is located at the center of the narrative. The egocentric nature of deixis is crucial to underline, in particular from a human development perspective, as this is key in understanding the interrelationships of language acquisition, spatial cognition, and development of empathy.

Deictic expressions are the frontiers in language acquisition; it is innate to humans to point to things first and then acquire the words that correspond to those expressions. In early childhood, during the acquisition of deictic expressions, psycholinguists observed strong egocentric bias.[9] Children are inclined to collapse deictic depth, both in person and place expressions, and initially lack the differentiation between what is close and what is far apart; or between what refers to them and to others. For instance, the difficulty in differentiating deictic contrasts and resorting to [here] and [this] even when the correct expression is [there] and [that] are the natural egocentric tendencies of this age group.

Eve Clark and C. Sengul's study on acquisition of deixis in children focuses on the spatial deictic terms of [here] and [this] as proximal terms, while [there] and [that] as non-proximal terms. They define the proximal and non-proximal contrast between each pair as "deictic contrast."[10] Based on experiments they conducted with nursery school children, Clark and Sengul argue that "children go through at least three stages in acquiring the deictic contrasts. They start with NO CONTRAST, work out a PARTIAL CONTRAST used only in certain contexts, and finally master a FULL CONTRAST equivalent to the adult's."[11] As their study shows, in the path to achieving full deictic contrast, children have to overcome both the "egocentric bias" that favors the choice of their words in relationship to themselves, and the "proximity bias" that favors being near the speaker.

According to Piaget's stages of cognitive development, children at the "Preoperational Stage" of development have a strong sense of egocentrism. He explains, "if the child sees everything from his own point of view, it is because he believes all the world to think like himself. He has not yet discovered the multiplicity of possible perspectives and remains blind to all but his own as if that were the only one possible."[12] Referring back to the diagram of deictic center as shown in Figure 3.2 and comparing it to Piaget's description of a child's egocentric point of view, we can draw strong parallels. The child plays the role of the speaker in their own world. The narrative is constructed from a single vantage point, and it does not allow the recognition of other perspectives.

An awareness of the egocentric nature of the deictic center is a crucial first step in designing for empathy and being able to shift it to consider the perspective of others. In other words, shifting from personal to external perspectives is a key strategy in creating an empathic environment.

The formation of our deictic center is situated in physical space and, therefore, it is coded in our spatial cognition. To better understand how we can create strategies to counter this egocentric framework, which has been embedded in our acquisition of language since early childhood, it is important to expand the discussion beyond deixis to spatial cognition. By understanding the relationship between deixis and spatial cognition we can shift the perspective from a single vantage point (egocentric) to others (allocentric).

EGOCENTRIC AND ALLOCENTRIC FRAMES OF REFERENCE

Spatial perspective, the home turf of architects, has also been, as Barbara Tversky points out, a focal point for scholars studying object recognition, environmental cognition, developmental psychology, neuropsychology, and language.[13] In the study of spatial cognition, the construct of the spatial perspective is defined in relation to a frame of reference that comes either from a viewer-centered (egocentric) or an external (allocentric) position. (Figure 3.3)

An egocentric frame of reference defines the location of things indexed to the first person's perspective, whereas in an allocentric frame of reference, the location of things is considered independent from the first person. It is defined in reference to other objects.[14]

Spatial frames of reference effectively inform of how we define, navigate, and establish relationships in our environment. We are all born into our egocentric frame of reference. As Michel Denis points out: "Each of us, with his/her own egocentric view of the world, interacts with other people who have their respective egocentric views of a shared environment. The question here is that of our capacity to adopt the perspective of other people."[17] Taking the perspective of other people does not come naturally to us, and it has a cognitive cost. But it is worth it, because, as Denis argues, "by combining together spatial information taken from different viewpoints, people will enjoy the possibility of forming richer representations of their environments."[18]

If we return to Piaget's stages of cognitive development theory, the egocentric frame of reference is how we first start to discover the world. As we get older, we learn to take other perspectives, but even then, our egocentric frame of reference continues to define our spatial perception. It is our cognitive short cut, or we might consider it our "default mode."

Defaults are powerful and ubiquitous in our lives, and they play a significant role in shaping our day-to-day behavior. According to Richard Thaler and Cass Sunstein, in order to move toward making better choices, we need to be "nudged"—a strategy that allows us to shift from a default mode, which

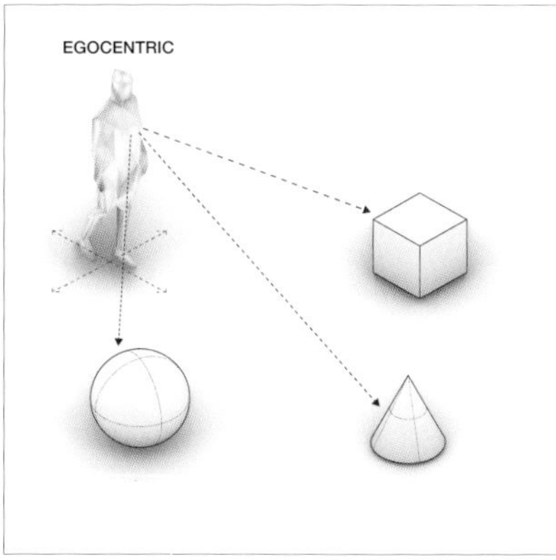

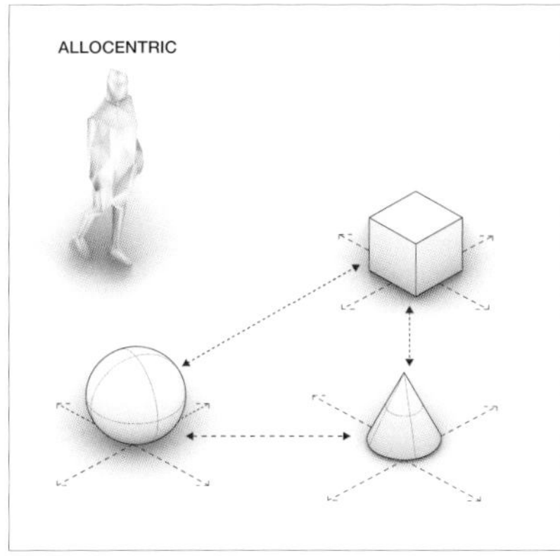

3.3 Spatial Frames of Reference.

"An egocentric reference frame is where one denotes the location of something else in reference to oneself. In contrast, an allocentric reference frame is where the location of something else is in reference to yet another object, independent of oneself." [15] Note that these diagrams do not show any spatial context, and in actuality, our spatial cognition operates on a much more complex context and our choices of spatial frame of references are influenced by the physical environment, such as the size of the space, its geometric structure and complexity, and the presence or absence of landmarks.[16]

favors the least path of cognitive resistance toward one that requires effort but offers us a more rewarding experience.[19] But what are these "nudges" that will allow us to shift from an egocentric frame of reference to an allocentric one? And, more specifically, what are they within the physical environment?

This question brings architectural discourse to the discussion. Since the spatial frames of reference define the nature of our perspective taking, and these frames of reference share the common spatial attributes with the physical (architectural) environment, I suggest that manipulating the construct of these spatial perspectives has the potential to help us shift perspectives. In other words, we could purposefully design "spatial nudges" to ease the cognitive cost toward adopting allocentric frames of reference. The significance of being able to shift the frame of reference goes beyond enriching spatial cognition; it is also how we can create a more empathic environment.

Barbara Tversky expands on the importance of shifting from our personal perspectives to, what she calls, a more neutral ground to foster social interaction:

> Individuals have different perspectives, not just on space, but on the events that take place in space. They also have different perspectives on beliefs, attitudes, and values. For the endless discussions people have on these topics, the mine-yours-neutral distinction is essential.

3.4 Avenues Silicon Valley, Parent Information Center. A series of portals creates a threshold moment for the entry experience.

> Reconciling my memory or beliefs or attitudes or values to yours might (or might not) best be accomplished by moving from personal to neutral ground. Going beyond personal perspective is as critical to social interaction as it is to spatial cognition.[20]

To discuss how to go beyond our personal perspective and find neutral ground for social interaction, we need to dissect the correlations between our deictic center and the spaces we occupy. In other words, the relationship between language and space.

PERCEPTUAL SPACE (P-SPACE) **AND LANGUAGE SPACE** (L-SPACE)

In the early stages of human development, our awareness of things or people outside ourselves is connected to the world that we can directly experience with our senses. Only the objects or people that are within this perspectival space exist, and when they disappear from that perspectival space, not only do they disappear from perception, but their entire existence seemingly vanishes. Early learning specialists correlate a baby getting upset and crying at a nursery during a parent drop-off with the understanding that for a baby, the disappearance of her parents from her sightline is associated with their loss from her life.

Consider this common occurrence: a baby sits in her highchair, and she throws an object, like her toy or spoon, on the floor. She starts crying when the object she just threw away disappeared from her sightline. An adult interferes with this situation and grabs the object from the floor, cleans it, and puts it back on her highchair. The baby smiles at first, and then throws the object back out again. In this scenario, the baby is not testing the parent's patience, but rather, she is learning something important. She is learning that [this] object in front of her continues to exist even when she throws it on the floor, which is outside of her sightline. The reappearance of the object with the assistance of an adult reassures the baby that the object that she threw away is still there even when she can no longer see it. Piaget calls the realization that something continues to exist—even when it's no longer sensed—"object permanence."[21] Even though the baby cannot talk, she uses gestures of pointing, as she cognitively develops object permanence. Before the acquisition of language, she uses the deictic gestures of being [here] and seeing [this] object.

As children start to talk, how do they acquire deixis in language—pointing with words—when they have encountered it, thus far, only by pointing their fingers? Unlike categorical words like "spoon" or names like "Joe" that do not change depending on who speaks and where they speak from, the correct use of deictic terms is dependent on the speaker's position and the proximity of the subject matter to the speaker.

In an essay on how a child acquires English expressions for space and time, psycholinguist Herbert H. Clark argues that the child acquires them "by learning how to apply these expressions to the a priori knowledge [that the child] has about space and time."[22] This a priori knowledge comes from a space Clark calls "P-space," the perceptual space the child is born into. He writes:

> The child is born into a flat world with gravity, and he himself is endowed with eyes, ears, an upright posture, and other biological structure. These structures alone lead him to develop a perceptual space, a P-space, with very specific properties. Later on, the child must learn how to apply English spatial terms to this perceptual space, and so the structure of P-space determines in large part what he learns and how he quickly learns it. The notion is that the child cannot apply some term correctly if he does not already have the appropriate concept in his P-space.[23]

As a baby discovers the phenomena of gravity that forces the objects she throws toward the floor, into disappearance from her vision, she is developing a broader world than her innate P-space, where objects exist beyond her immediate vision (object permanence). The baby expresses herself using deictic expressions in absence of spoken language. As she acquires the language expressions that relate to the concepts of P-space, she enters what Clark calls "L-space," the concept of space underlying English spatial terms. L-space coincides with P-space, as such that "any property found in L-space should also be found in P-space."[24]

Clark summarizes the characteristics of the P-space of a person, in upright position—what he calls the canonical position—as "the optimal position to perceive other objects visually, auditorily, tactually, etc."[25] And he defines these in geometric terms: "P-space consists of three reference planes and three associated directions: (1) ground level is a reference plane and upward is positive; (2) the vertical left-to-right plane through the body is another reference plane and forward from the body is positive; and (3) the vertical front-to-back plane is the third reference plane and leftward and rightward are both positive directions."[26] (Figure **3.6**)

3.5 (Facing page) Avenues Shenzhen Campus, exterior playground.

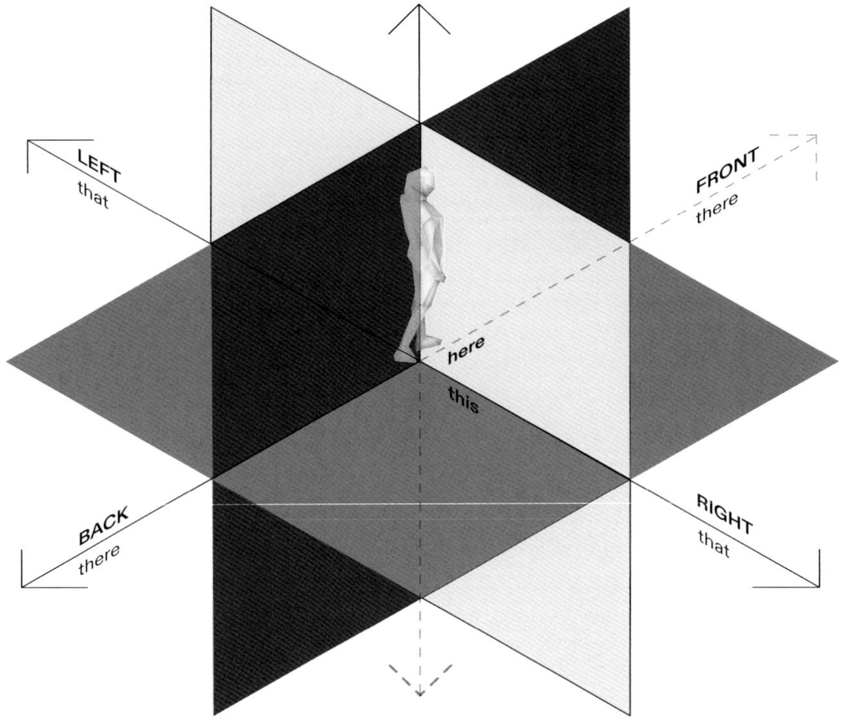

3.6 P-Space. The diagram is created based on Herbert Clark's definition.

According to Clark, "the perceptual features in the child's early cognitive development (his P-space) are reflected directly in the semantics of his language (his L-space)."[27] The critical role that the P-space plays in the development of the individual's L-space is an important hinge in the interrelationship between deixis, architecture, and empathy. P-space is innate to the person's experience; it is phenomenological; and it is directly relatable to the physical environment. Architects shape the P-space, and as such, they have an influence on the development of the L-space for both the individual and society. Therefore, in theory, if we can design the P-space purposefully, we can shift the semantics (meaning) and potentially create a place that catalyzes empathy. This is the premise of this chapter, and the design conjectures included later in the chapter illustrate how, with my design team, I have explored these relationships in our projects. But first, it is important to discuss the theoretical framework that acts as a bridge between psycholinguistics and architectural discourse.

DEIXIS AND PROJECTIVE GEOMETRY

Deixis is contextual. As previously outlined, all forms of deictic words and expressions are dependent on anchoring a point in time, space, and a person. There is foreground and background, there is a vantage point, a perspectival hinge, in deictic words.[28] Deixis is where language enters perspectival space. And this is the space where it shares a common ground with architecture: geometry.

Robin Evans, in his seminal work *The Projective Cast: Architecture and Its Three Geometries*, underlines the indispensable role that geometry plays, "a constitutive part of Architecture."[29] Evans points out that the first place we encounter geometry in architecture is in the shape of the buildings. As we look at a building, we start reading it in geometric terms—it may be a circular building or a pyramid, for example. Another obvious place to see geometry is in the drawings of buildings. We all encounter architectural drawings, whether we are design professionals or not, perhaps in a guidebook while sightseeing, or in the fire exit plan attached at the back of our hotel door, or the floor plans real estate agents share for the house we are considering buying. Evans calls this geometry "stolid and dormant," in other words: useful but dead. It helps us to be informed but does not allow spatial perception nor does it bring us into perspectival space. Projective geometry is where this happens.

Evans mapped out a diagram to show the permeation of projections in architecture, illustrating multiple fields of projections between different targets. (Figure 3.7) He envisioned this diagram to be flowing from any of the five target points, taking ten possible routes to illustrate how the projective geometry is at play at various stages of design, documentation, construction, and experience of the architectural space.

The set of projections that occur when a person experiences a building is perhaps the least abstract of the projections defined in Evans's diagram. Any person walking within a physical environment is in perspectival space and the sensory information that surrounds her is mapped into her perception as indicated with path #7. Within the perspectival space, a person is also standing at her deictic center, as her anchor point, when she communicates with another person, or points out to things. For instance, if she decides to

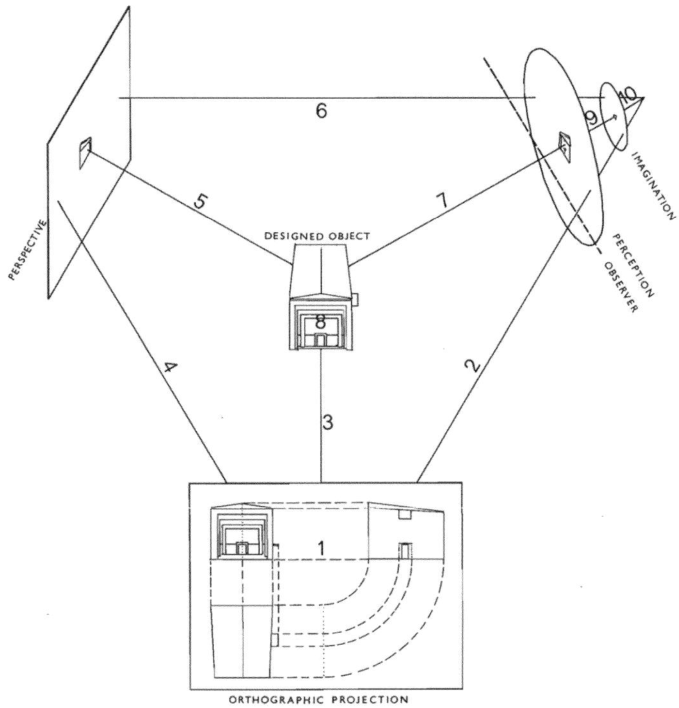

3.7 Projection and its analogues. Diagram by Robin Evans, as published in *The Projective Cast: Architecture and Its Three Geometries.*

take a photograph of another person standing further, she will be pointing the camera from her deictic center toward [him]. With this photograph she has just created a perspectival drawing of [him] as he is standing [there]. And the perspectival drawing (photograph) she created will be another type of projection (as seen in path #5), one that flattens three dimensionality onto a screen. If her friend standing [there] points to the photograph, referring to it as "[that] photograph," he also speaks from his own deictic center (as seen in path #6). As we can see, in this simple vignette, a set of architectural projections occurs in parallel with a set of deictic projections.

Evans draws a dashed line at the observer, and according to him this line represents a separation between the world and the self, the objective and the subjective.[30] Imagination and visual perception (paths #9 and #10) occur in this subjective world of the observer. In other words, this is where the observer develops her representations of the world.

Evans argues that geometry is indispensable to architecture. Similarly, geometry is indispensable to deictics, as they operate within the same perspectival space, governed by the same rules of projective geometry.

Let's consider the point in time when the architect is in the process of designing a building. The architect uses orthogonal projections, perspectival drawings, and scale models during the design process. The projective geometry rules that govern the experience of architecture are the same ones at play during the design process. For instance, when an architect draws sketches to represent her imaginations, she is using a set of projections between her imagination and the two-dimensional drawing she has just created (as seen in path #2). Likewise, a scale model or a perspectival drawing are also different modes of representation that are governed by the principles of projective geometry. However, these principles that are integral to the design process do not always manifest themselves explicitly in the experience of the completed building. This is because the principles of projective geometry are often reduced to instruments of documentation. There are examples though, where the architectural expression of the building celebrates its genesis through projective geometry.

The Philips Pavilion designed by Le Corbusier in collaboration with composer Iannis Xenakis for Expo '58 in Brussels is a fine example of that. (Figure 3.8) Even though this exhibition pavilion was a temporary structure, it was a pivotal work during Le Corbusier's late career. It shows a mastery of geometry in using hyperbolic shells, and moreover, according to Kenneth Frampton, it is the culmination of Le Corbusier's preoccupation both with electronic music and with the ideal of the "total work of art." During the design process, Le Corbusier "commissioned Varèse to write a multi-track electronic score that would accompany the 480-second kinetic light display, he himself selected the images for this spectacle and controlled the pattern of colored filters to be superimposed over the projections. This schedule, together with the script, determined the coordinated sequence of images and sounds to be projected against the complex curvature of the hyperbolic shell vaults which constituted the body of the Philips Pavilion."[31]

In the Philips Pavilion, the lines that define the hyperbolic paraboloid surfaces offer the viewer the experience of both the physical manifestation of the

3.8 The Philips Pavilion at the 1958 Brussels World Fair.

building and its underlining tectonic definitions. The conspicuous geometric definition of the hyperbolic surfaces that is observed both inside and outside are the lines of the prestressing cables that hold the precast concrete segments in place, and which together constitute the shells. Designed and constructed with a clear understanding of projective geometry, this unusual structure celebrates its design philosophy, which sprung from bringing the rhythmic structure of music and syncopations of light projections, in both the design and experience of architecture. Even seeing it through photographs today, one is transformed into an experience of projections that pull us into a broader intellectual discourse.[32] It prompts us to ask questions about music and architecture. We have left our individual perspective and now become part of a conversation on *Gesamtkunstwerk* (total work of art).[33]

INTO THE SPACE OF PROJECTIONS

I have always been fascinated by being able to trace the lines of projections while experiencing architecture. The source of my fascination, I believe, is rooted in the congruity between the a priori rules of perception and the intellectual framework of design that has shaped the physical environment I occupy at that moment. In such an environment, we are transformed from the momentous experience of being in that space, at that time, as an individual, to understanding the process of making that space, including all the intellectual perspectives that went into that making. The significant potency of this transformation is hinged on the transformation of our spatial cognition—shifting it from an egocentric to an allocentric frame of reference—through the use of projective geometry.

Development studies of early childhood have demonstrated that our first mode of experiencing the world is through an egocentric perspective. Even after we develop the ability to take other perspectives, the egocentric frame of reference is embedded within us, as our natural base and our default. The egocentric frame of reference defines our individuality and thus, it is critical to maintain it as a unique notion of who we are. But without learning to take other perspectives, we cannot create healthy social interactions. In the process of learning to take other perspectives, the physical environment plays an important role. And in the experience of the physical environment, the forces of projective geometry are inherent. The resonance between our egocentric frame of reference—with its vanishing point in the perspectival space—and a physical environment that allows us to experience other projections while looking through our egocentric frame of reference, creates a powerful transformation—one that allows us to shift perspectives. Therefore, in the pursuit of designing for empathy, I will highlight those design concepts that celebrate the congruity between the forces that impact our spatial perception and the rules of projective geometry that form the spaces we occupy.

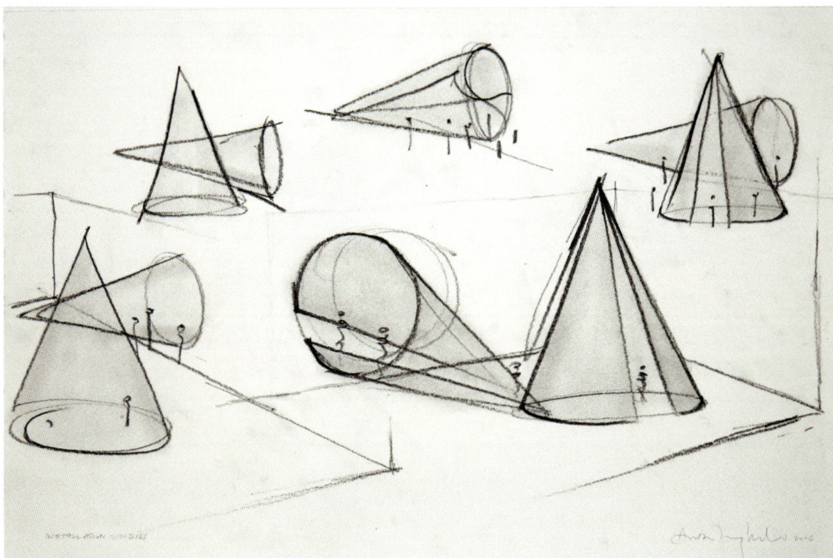

3.9 (Top) Anthony McCall, *Line Describing a Cone;* (bottom) McCall's sketches for solid light films.

3.10 Albrecht Dürer, Man *Drawing a Lute* (1525), which depicts a perspective machine, woodcut print 1525.

DESIGNING WITH PROJECTIONS

While watching—or perhaps more appropriately "being within"—Anthony McCall's film *Line Describing a Cone*, one experiences inhabiting a projective geometry drawing-in-construction.[34] And this is the artist's intention. According to McCall, his film "exist only in the present: the moment of projection."[35] The film takes place in a three-dimensional space, a completely dark room with all surfaces painted black. The walls, ceiling, and floor of the room merge into a seemingly boundless space. The boundaries of the room are not the point, as we are meant to be in an abstract space. There is a constant mist of smoke in the air that is released intermittently from an invisible source, making a hissing sound and sending patterns of smoke into the light beams coming from a projector. The projector slowly draws a point becoming a circle on a black screen which in the three-dimensional space makes a line, slowly completing a cone. The smoke solidifies the light beams, defining the surfaces of the projections. Meanwhile, the visitors that interact with the installation interrupt the conical projection and insert their own projections. They become part of the installation. (Figure **3.9**, top)

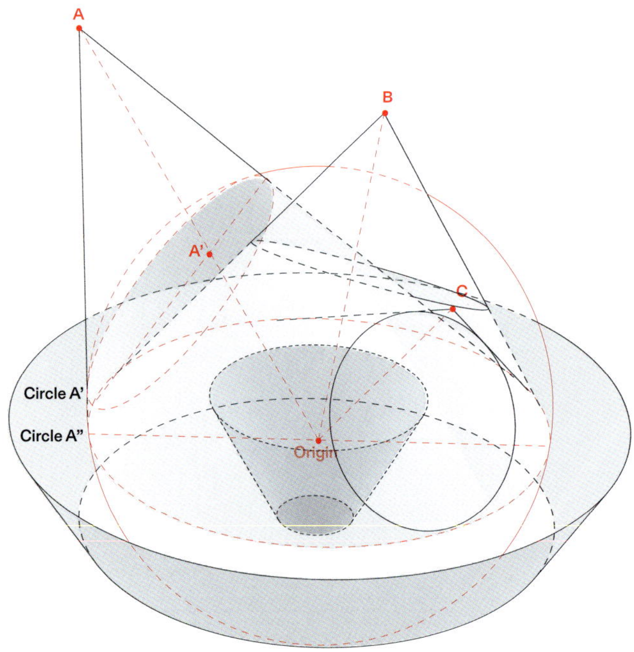

3.11 Doha Art Pavilion. Diagram showing the three conical projections of the roof and the inverse conical projection of the reflecting pool.

The film as a medium in McCall's work is not perceived on a screen, but it happens in an in-between space, somewhere between the projector and the screen—the "space of projections."

One of the earliest illustrations of the "space of projections" dates back to the sixteenth century, in Albrecht Dürer's depiction of a perspective machine (Figure 3.10). By demonstrating how the lines of projections flatten three dimensionality onto paper, thus creating an image of that three-dimensional object seen from a vantage point, Dürer's machine shows how to correctly construct a perspectival drawing. By contrast, McCall's film puts us inside the perspective machine, into the space of projections, and thus makes the vantage point irrelevant. Its irrelevancy, though, is not because the vantage point disappears; in fact, it does not. The 16-mm projector is placed as the only physical object in the room, reminding us of its presence. What becomes important is not the image projected on the screen, but our experience of the projection process. In other words, in McCall's film, the visual construct from a single vantage point is proliferated to multiple vantage points, and by this our spatial experience shifts away from its egocentric frame of reference.

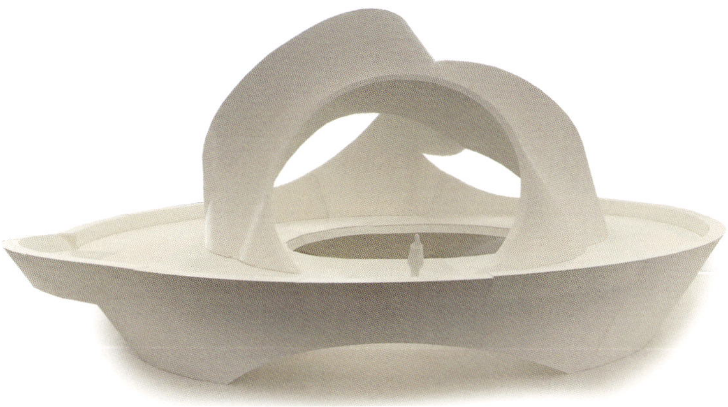

3.12 Doha Art Pavilion, physical model.

Inspired by McCall's films, we created a space defined by conical projections for a small art pavilion project in Doha. The three cones that frame the sky are countered by an inverse cone from a reflective pool opening toward the sky. (Figure **3.11**) The interplay of the conical projections puts the observer in a space of projections, juxtaposing the individual's cone of vision with the multiple conical projections that define the space.

3.13 Interior view of the Doha Art Pavilion showing the juxtapositions of conical projections that can be experienced from a single vantage point.

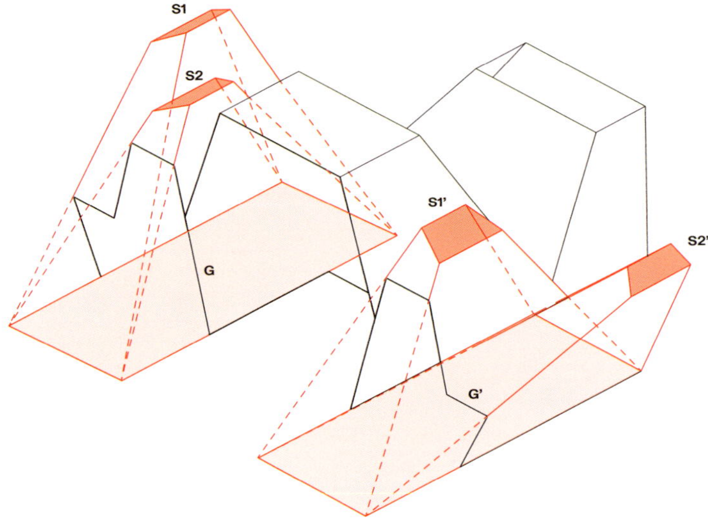

3.14 Kaunas Concert Hall diagram of projections illustrating the light cones.

The power of these juxtapositions allows the individual to let go of their personal cone of vision defined by their vantage point, to wander into the other cones that define the space around them. The resulting space offers multiple perspectival hinges, to be experienced from a single vantage point. (Figure 3.13)

We further explored using projective geometry, as both the genesis concept and the final manifestation of the design, for a concert hall project in Kaunas, Lithuania. Whereas the conical projections of the Doha pavilion framed the sky, water, and the city, for this project we focused on tracing the light in the space by shrinking the opening size and creating a darker environment. As seen in Figure 3.14, a source plane (S1) is projected down to a target plane (G). Similarly, a second source plane (S2) is projected down to the same target plane (G). The intersection of these two projection cones forms the physical boundaries of space. Both source planes (S1) and (S2) are skylights. Target plane (G) is is illuminated by the light coming through the skylight planes. The resultant intersecting volume is cast in concrete, in effect turning the ephemeral lines of projections into the hard edges of the concrete surfaces. As daylight moves through these spaces, the angle of the sun will at times align with the projection cone.

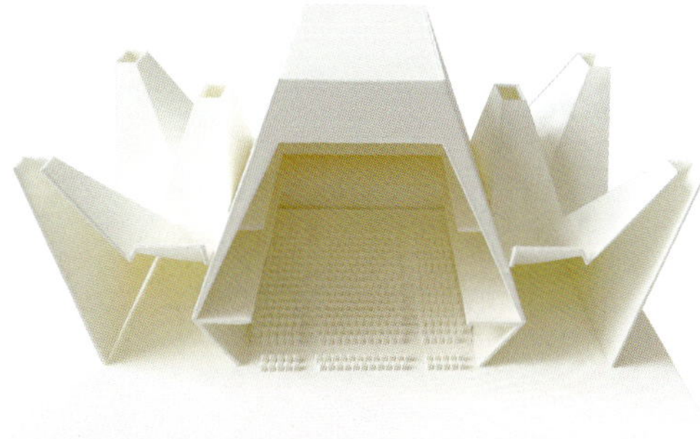

3.15 Kaunas Concert Hall, study models.

At these moments, the cone will be activated with light. At other times of day, the light will create additional projections on the walls of the cones. When the rays of the sun do not directly come through the skylight opening, exterior ambient diffuse light will bring gradient brightness from the skylight planes down toward the ground plane. The tracing of light into these cones throughout the day resonates with the projective cast of the concrete that defines the spaces.

The geometric construct illustrated in Figure 3.15, forms the tectonic integer of the project that is repeated in variations of scale and orientation throughout the building to create a field condition. The intersecting volumes of these multiple projection cones create the spatial syntax of the project. The location of the skylight frames and the angle of projection is calibrated to the solar movement, to give each space a unique light quality. The geometric intricacies created by the intersecting light projections cast in concrete become the architectural expression of the building, experienced both inside and out. Similar to the Philips Pavilion in its intentional use of projective geometry as both the genesis and the experience of architecture, this project attempts to shift the individual's perspective toward a deeper appreciation of space, sculpted by light.

3.16 Kaunas Concert Hall, interior rendering.

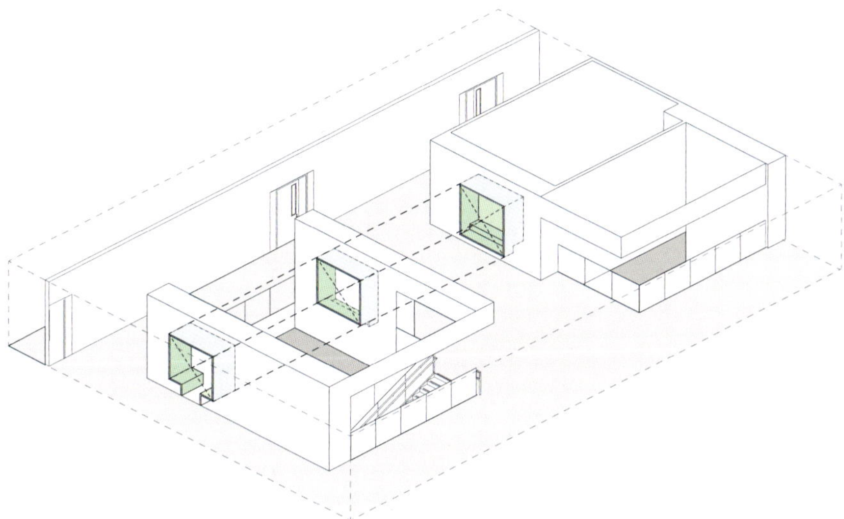

3.18 Three niches conjecture

VISUAL ECHO IN THE PERSPECTIVAL SPACE
(PERSONAL-DEIXIS AND EMPATHY)

Using the construction lines of projective geometry as the generative concept for space-making, as seen in the Doha Art Pavilion and the Kaunas Concert Hall projects, offers a strong connection between the rules of design and the rules of perception. The edges that define the spaces in these projects are also the same lines that our perception works to construct its own projections. The building almost creates a set of perspectival drawings, carefully choreographed for the onlooker to experience. Taking this design strategy into the design of learning environments offers a valuable asset in making the connections between the P-space and its counterpart L-space, as defined by Herbert Clark. My theory is that spatial deictic words like [here], [there], [this], or [that] and personal deictic words like [I/we], [you], or [he/she/they] can be acquired by children easier in a space that deliberately constructs the deictic depth in the P-space. As seen in Figure 3.18, the construct of the P-space can make proximity and non-proximity explicit and hence the correlation between the language and the space can be made more direct.

3.17 (Facing page) Avenues Shenzhen Early Learning Center three niches conjecture.

3.19 Three niches conjecture diagrams showing different locations of first person and the relative positioning of the second and third person.

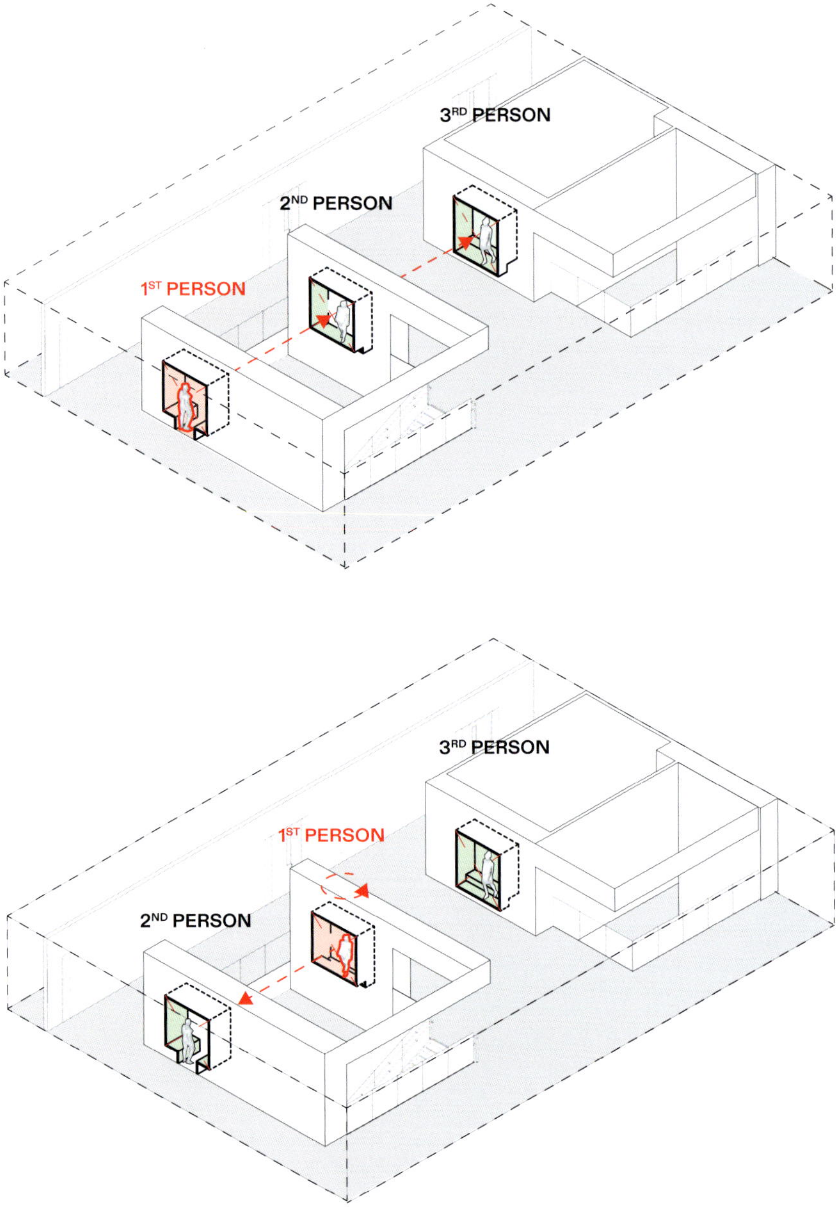

For Avenues Early Learning Center project in Shenzhen, we created a purposefully choreographed series of niche spaces for the students. Here, three identical frames are arranged on the same axis, across a space that is open to below. Each frame creates a seating niche, lined with the same green fabric, marking its presence clearly within its respective white wall. The niches look almost identical with small variations. The first one, shown in the foreground, has a keyhole shape and features a writable glass surface that allows for a visual connection to the double-height atrium below. The middle niche also features writable glass, but its shape is square. The third niche, which is the farthest away in Figure 3.17 and visible only through the middle niche, is open to the student commons located in front of it and has a solid back wall.

All three frames create their own deictic centers but share the same axial arrangement of a single-point perspective. This creates a strong visual connection between each of these individual deictic centers. But the critical element of this design is the visual echo, created by the "three-niches" arrangement. For the children in the foreground, their perspective-taking—based on their own deictic center—is contextualized by the students directly across from them. In the acquisition of personal deictic words like [I] or [we], the impact of the three niches P-space on the cognitive development of the children is to help develop an awareness of the perspective of [others] that co-exist with them in the same perspectival space. Such awareness can catalyze empathy in learning environments. In broader terms, by facilitating the acquisition of language in a specially constructed P-space, we can encourage a shift in the egocentric bias of young children toward a more empathic worldview.

Derived from our design study at Avenues Early Learning Center, the "three niches" conjecture is a P-space construct that assists with the acquisition of deictic expressions with empathy in early childhood. The three niches conjecture is constructed as follows: Define three deictic centers and locate them on the same perspectival axis, the positive and negative directions of each being parallel to the axis. On each deictic center, the vertical front-to-back perpendicular plane of the person is visually framed with an identical or similar marker to achieve a visual echo. The framing elements should have conspicuous geometric, textural, and color similarities. (See Figure 3.17)

If the grammatical first person is located on the deictic center at either end of the axis, all the three personas can be subsequently located in the same direction. This type of arrangement for the P-space will result in the construction of second and third person for the L-space, and hence the perspective taking can be expanded to the [other] in the same directional axis. If the grammatical first person is located in the middle, the second person is visible across, whereas the third person will be behind the first person, or toward the negative direction. The first person located in the middle will need to pivot to visually engage with the third person. (Figure **3.19**)

The forced perspective construct of the three niches conjecture creates three egocentric reference frames that align toward the same vanishing point. The visual echo of each frame is intended to catalyze perspective taking for each individual, shifting the focus of spatial cognition to social interaction. In this specially choreographed P-space, which allows multiple perspectives in the same narrative, a shift from an egocentric frame of reference to an allocentric frame of reference is intended.

VISUAL COUNTERPOINT IN THE PERSPECTIVAL SPACE
(TIME-DEIXIS AND EMPATHY)

Raphael's fresco *The School of Athens* (1509–1511) is located in the Stanze di Raffaello (1508) a series of richly illustrated reception rooms in the Apostolic Palace in the Vatican. *The School of Athens* is famous for its perspectival depth, which, particularly when seen within the context of the room, offers an interesting point of view on time deixis—the fourth dimension of the deictic center's geometric construct. When we stand straight in front of Raphael's fresco we look into a perfectly constructed perspectival space. (Figure **3.20**, left)

In our P-space, the positive time axis represents the front, meaning [tomorrow] is yet to come ahead. And yet, the figures of Aristotle and Plato are walking toward us. The deictic future of the ancient Greek philosophers runs in the geometrically opposite direction from our own deictic future. The visual counterpoint between our perspectival vantage point and that of the philosophers creates a mirroring of time deixis. Embedded within the beauty

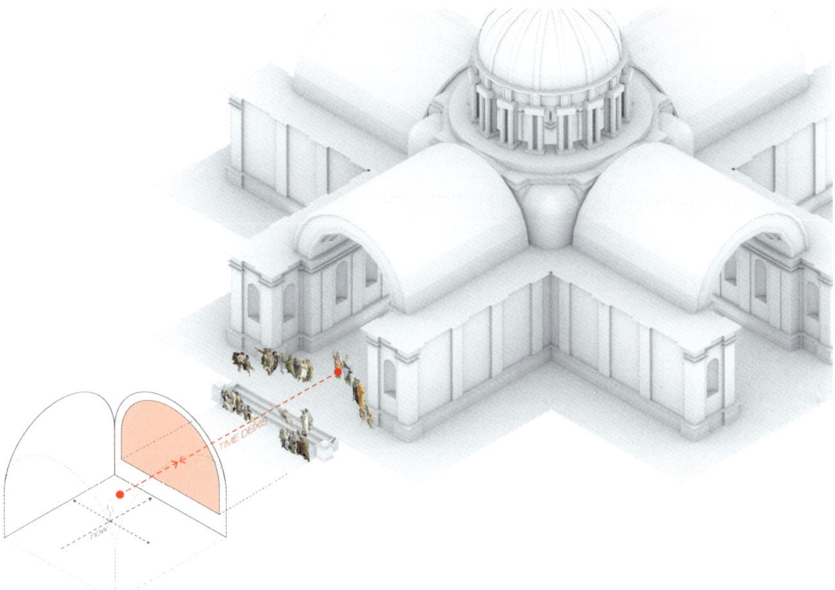

3.20 (Above left) *The School of Athens*, Raphael (1509–1511). (Above right) The fresco is located on the east wall of the Stanza della Segnatura, one of the four Raphael Rooms in the Apostolic Palace in the Vatican.

3.21 (Left) Reciprocal time axes between the observer and the philosophers: The diagram shows the observer within the Stanze di Raffaello and the three-dimensional setting of *The School of Athens.*

of his painting, Raphael created a purposeful construct: a portal through time for intellectual empathy.

If we step back from our frontal position in order to get a view of the overall room, we will notice that the arch that carefully frames the fresco also supports the dome of the room we're standing in. (Figure 3.20, right) [Today], inside the fifteenth-century building, as we stand in front of this Renaissance fresco, looking into an ancient Greek scene, we exist in a purposefully constructed P-space where time gains new meaning in our L-space.

The scene at Stanze di Raffaello and Raphael's masterful trompe l'oeil offer a valuable design strategy. The visual counterpoint between the perspective of the individual observer and the perspective of the painting, in a setting that has a strong visual echo between the architecture of the room and the architecture depicted in the painting, causes a reciprocity between the time axis of the observer's deictic center and the philosophers' deictic centers. It is this reciprocity that allows us to have a deeper understanding of context.

Context is critical to the discussion on designing for empathy. Architects always work within existing contexts, and everything we add, relative to what is already there, is always new. The question of how and what we do in that existing context is an important one to consider, especially when the existing context includes historically significant buildings. In these contexts, it becomes even more critical that our interventions create spatial conditions that foster allocentric frames of reference through which a meaningful co-existence can occur.

Efficiency Lab's proposal for the New Contemporary Art Wing and Education Center at the Lima Art Museum is located within such a context, rich with historical and cultural layers. The design brief for this project required an expansion to the existing museum housed in the nineteenth-century Exposition Palace, a neo-classical building designed by Italian architect Antonio Leonardi, who was living in Lima at the time. The program requirement was to build a respectable relationship with the historical building by locating most of the expansion spaces below grade, limiting any above-grade presence to building entrances only. Any physical engagements with the historical building were to be avoided.

To create a below-grade expansion to the current museum without impacting the historical structure (below or above grade), resulted in a careful exploration of how to spatially connect the two buildings without any physical connections. In order to create an architecture of connections-without-touching we explored design strategies that would create a visual counterpoint to the historical building through the use of projections. The solid and void rhythm of the Exposition Palace's neoclassical west facade was projected onto the site, from which we generated the cadence of the corresponding lightwells and sunken gardens that run perpendicular to the historic building. (Figure 3.24) The translation of the architectural language of the Exposition Palace into rhythmic, meandering concrete forms creates a strong dialogue between the two structures; they connect without touching.

3.22 Lima Art Museum Expansion. Close up view of the portals facing the Exposition Palace.

3.23 (Following spread) Concrete portals in the Lima Art Museum Expansion frame the windows of the historic Exposition Palace.

The deliberate use of projective geometry as a design process creates conspicuous perspectival spaces as portals of connection—not only between the two buildings, but also between time—so that the contemporary expansion

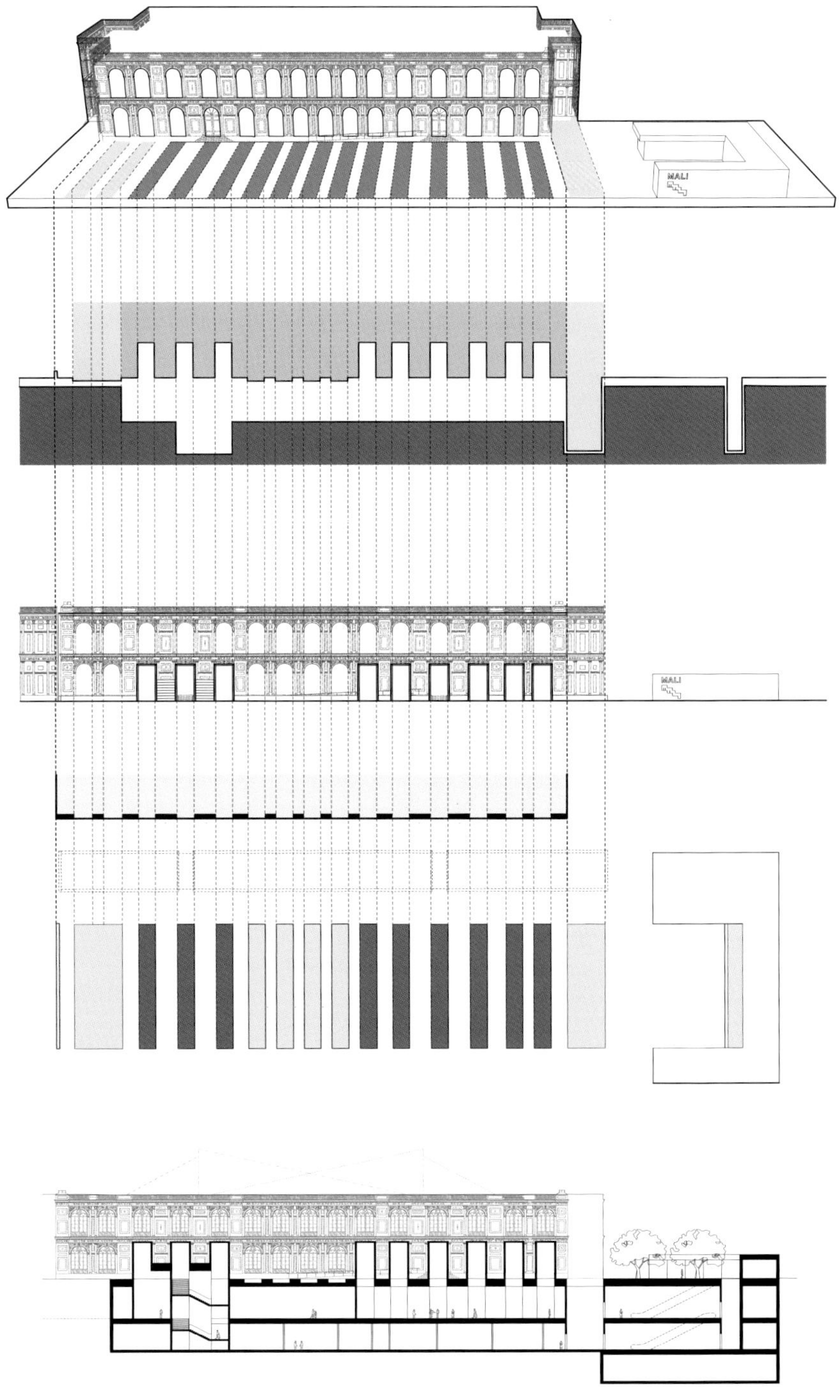

3.24 Diagram showing the design concept of the expansion to the Lima Art Museum based on using projective geometry. The facade articulation of the Exposition Palace is projected both in plan and section on the expansion site. Note the counterpoint between the facade rhythm of the historical building and the portals of the new expansion.

3.25 View of the crevasse between the new expansion and the historical building. The monolithic cascading levels descending along the facade of the historical building create a sense of foundation to it.

[now] can coexist with the original nineteenth-century building [then]. Just as Raphael's *The School of Athens* creates a reciprocal time deixis between the observer and the painting, the portals of the new expansion building reciprocate with the Exposition Palace, to culturally bridge across [now] and [then], so they can be synchronous in the same place.

However, we wanted to connect further than the nineteenth-century [then]; we wanted to connect [before then] with the pre-colonial culture in Peru, to the stereotomic architecture of Inca. To achieve that, the project proposes a crevasse between the new expansion and the Exposition Palace, creating a below-grade monolithic landform that defines a layered sectional cut, running along the existing building. It almost acts like a foundation to the nineteenth-century structure, suggesting that the new expansion has been there long before [then], flipping the time sequence of [now] to become [before then].

The echoes of the Exposition Palace resonate throughout the new extension at varying scales and levels. Looking up from the new galleries, visitors see the framed views of each corresponding bay of the historical facade. Coming from the sunken gardens, visitors see the grandeur of the historic building stretching the entire length of the monolithic crevasse. Shifting the center of the time deixis with the lines of projective geometry, the proposal creates an empathic public space, where the contemplation of the cultural heritage of [then] through the contemporary interventions of [now] with the awareness of [before then] is possible.

INVERTING THE DEICTIC CENTER, AND EMPATHY THROUGH AWARENESS

As discussed previously, the deictic center locates the first person at the center of the construct, making it an inherently egocentric frame of reference. In both design strategies discussed to counter this egocentric bias—the visual echo and the visual counterpoint—the concept of juxtaposition plays a key role in perspective taking and helps us move toward a deeper understanding of people, time, and space, consequently allowing a more empathic environment. For instance, in the three niches conjecture, the first, second, and third person are juxtaposed on the same deictic axis, encouraging us to see the point of view of the other. On the other hand, the visual counterpoint discussed for the Lima Museum project allows us to relate through different layers of historical contexts within the same space.

What if we invert the deictic center, and instead of putting the first person at the center of the construct, we put the object at the center, and thus allowing the nonhuman object to construct its own narratives? This conceptual shift will create a third spatial frame of reference, different from the egocentric and allocentric frames of references, both of which are based on human-centric points of view and carry the contextual bias of the time and place in which the narrative is constructed. By contrast, a spatial frame of reference that locates a non-human object as the anchor gives an autonomy to the object, allowing it to construct its own narratives. I call this concept an "isocentric frame of reference." The object in an isocentric frame of reference has the agency to construct its own deictic center through projections toward the first person's deictic center. (Figure 3.26, right) The potential to construct different juxtapositions within each of these projections will allow us to build multiple narratives for the same object, deepening our understanding of it.

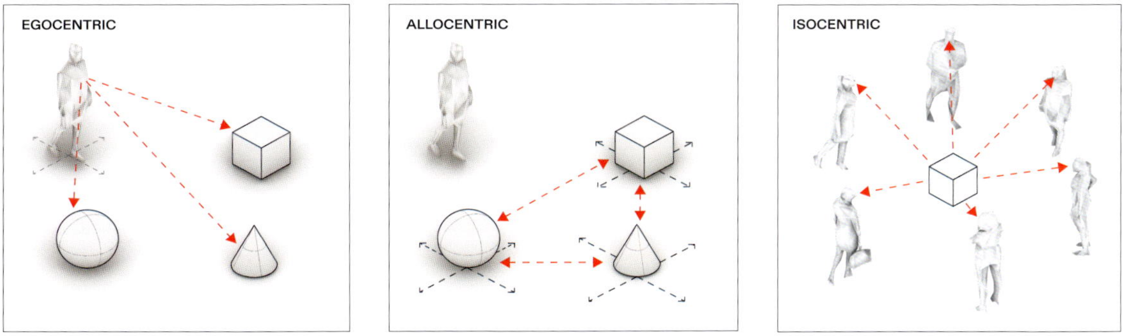

The next project creates a device that constructs an isocentric frame of reference for a historical artifact, allowing us to build both emotional and cognitive empathy toward the socio-political circumstances and consequences of the time the object was constructed and, subsequently, subverted. Furthermore, the juxtapositions within the spatial construct allow us to deepen our understanding of ongoing conflicts and their respective consequences to society and the environment.

3.26 Comparison of the three spatial frames of reference. Isocentric frame of reference, added to the egocentric and allocentric frames of reference as a new way to conceptualize pluralistic narratives.

Kowsky Plaza, located along the Battery Park City Esplanade in New York, is a small pocket park that contains a seemingly circumstantial assemblage of public attractions such as a dog park, a children's playground, a volleyball court, New York City Police Memorial, and a segment of the Berlin wall. The Berlin Wall segment was given to the Battery Park City Authority in 2004 by the German Consulate, and today sits on the Eastern Edge of the park, uncomfortably close to an apartment building, paradoxically surrounded by a metal picket fence. Most park visitors stroll past it without even recognizing it.

Concerned about the deterioration of the mural on the wall segment due to its decades-long exposure to varying weather conditions, the Battery Park City Authority issued a request for proposals from architects to design a protective envelope in 2022. The pragmatic concern of paint deterioration and the discussions to find solutions for preservation inadvertently brings us into deeper questions of what this object represents, how we should preserve it, what kind of relationship should we have with it and what kind of

3.27 Segment of Berlin Wall behind a picket fence in Kowsky Plaza.

relationship should it have with us, and notwithstanding, how it should sit at the eastern corner of Kowsky Plaza.

The Berlin Wall, the most recognizable symbol of the Cold War, was, of course, more than a wall; it was a series of walls, fences, a vehicle ditch, traps, observation towers, and a zone ominously named the "death strip," separating East and West Berlin. The segment of the wall that sits at Kowsky Plaza was originally located along the Kreuzberg neighborhood in Berlin, and the mural on the wall was painted by the French artist Thierry Noir in 1984. Noir's abstract minimalistic outlines with few colors grew out of the pragmatic realities of finishing the painting quickly without being caught by East German border guards. When Noir started painting the murals, at first, the West Berliners were suspicious; they took it as some sort of propaganda activity, but later embraced the murals. He was joined by other artists. For Noir, this act of defiance was a subversion of a war barrier into a humanistic canvas. As he stated, the act of painting the murals made him stronger than the wall itself.[36]

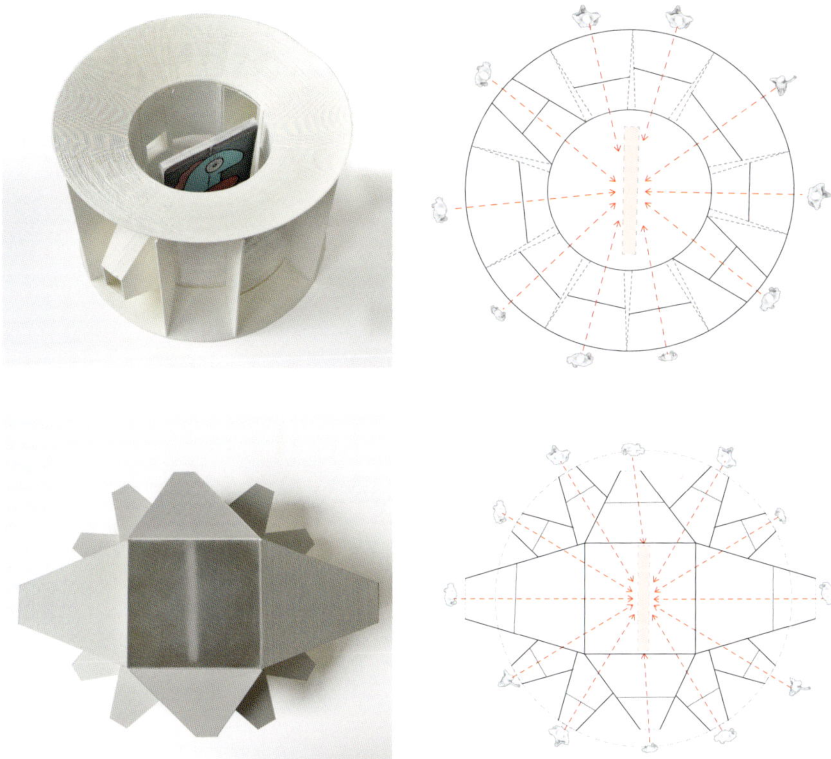

3.28 Two different schemes of the isocentric frame of reference. The Berlin Wall fragment is located at the center, illustrated with the red rectangle.

But what does his act of defiance, this subversive transformation of a Cold War apparatus into a humanistic artifact mean today, when a piece of it sits at the corner of a pocket park in Manhattan surrounded by a picket fence? In its new context, is it reduced to just a memento, a souvenir brought to New York City from another time and place?

As my office contemplated the Battery Park City Authority's requirement to create a shelter for this segment of Berlin Wall, we asked ourselves how we can redefine the dual narratives of humanity—oppressive and liberating—represented by the canvas and its painting. How could we reterritorialize this complicated piece of history in its new context and give it a voice that elevates it from an object of consumption as in a souvenir; transforming it into something that can bring us a heightened awareness of socio-political

3.29 Plane Ⓐ shown in the diagram is located at each deictic axis and the juxtaposed stories are placed on these planes.

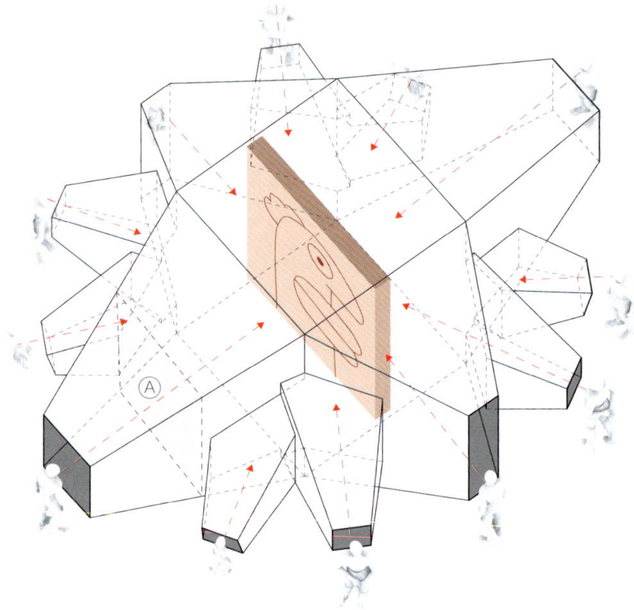

events of past and present? Our design proposal constructs an apparatus that locates the segment of the wall within an isocentric frame of reference. We designed two versions of the same concept. The first one is based on pure radial projections. The other option recognizes the cardinal axes of the wall and introduces the radial projections inserted in between them. (Figure 3.28) Both are manifestations of the same concept, even though they have different formal expressions.

In both schemes, the individual deictic centers for each person looking to the wall sees a framed view of the mural. The carefully curated perspectives toward the wall are in fact part of the isocentric projections of the wall, constructing its own narratives. Along each deictic axis, a frame is constructed to juxtapose on other narratives. The new narratives on these frames are intended to be temporary exhibits that will be curated by other artists that reflect their own conceptualization of the wall. (Figure 3.29, Plane A) In other words, they will be layering over Noir's painting, creating yet another form of subversion of the wall.

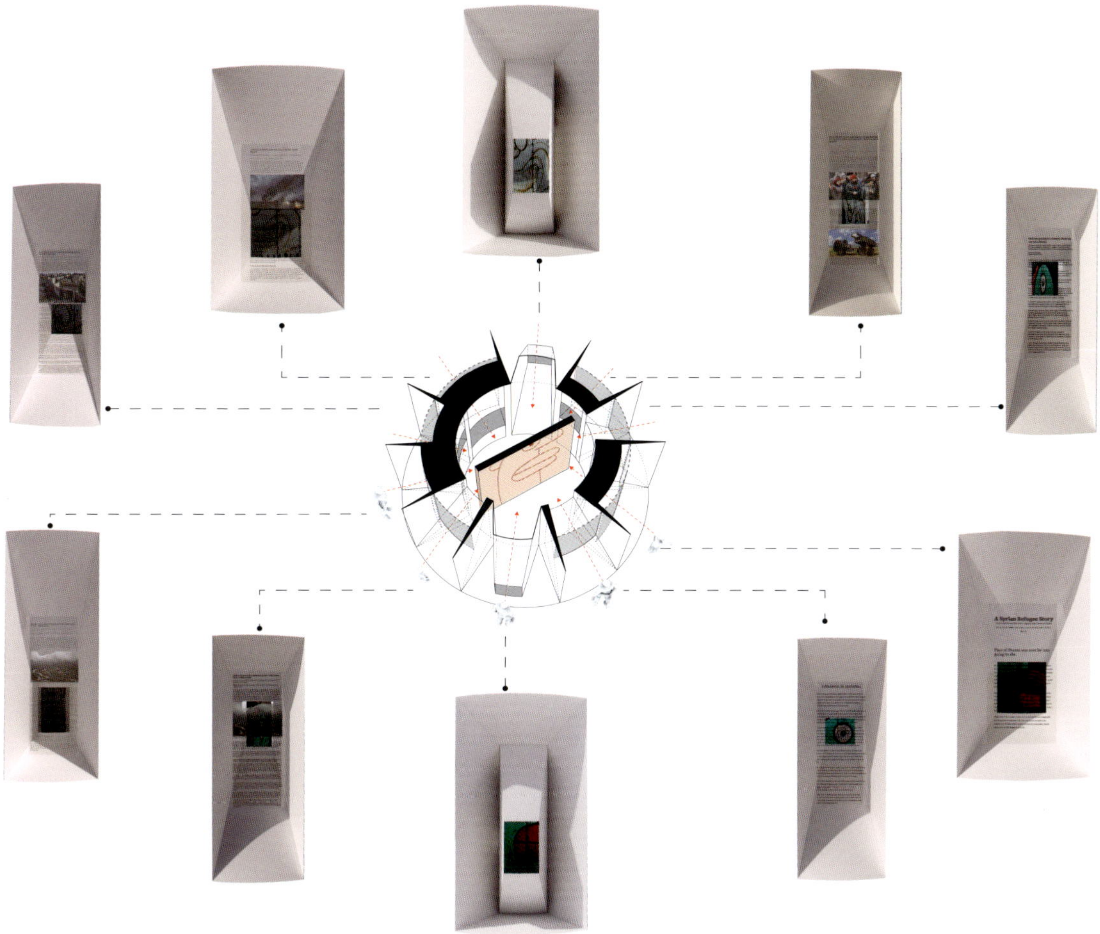

To illustrate how juxtapositions work at the isocentric frame of reference, we have curated one story line. Figure 3.31 shows one of the perspectives of the wall juxtaposed by the image and story of the Syrian refugees trying to cross the Aegean Sea on makeshift boats in 2015. In this particular image, we see a little boy who tragically drowned and washed out to the beach. The eye of the mural is looking toward us as we look back at it. And there is the little boy, lying motionless on our deictic axis. In this juxtaposition, Noir's drawing of the big eye is looking at the little boy, witnessing another human tragedy, on another death strip—in this case an Ancient Sea transformed into one.

3.30 Isocentric frames of reference, multiple narratives juxtaposed on each deictic center.

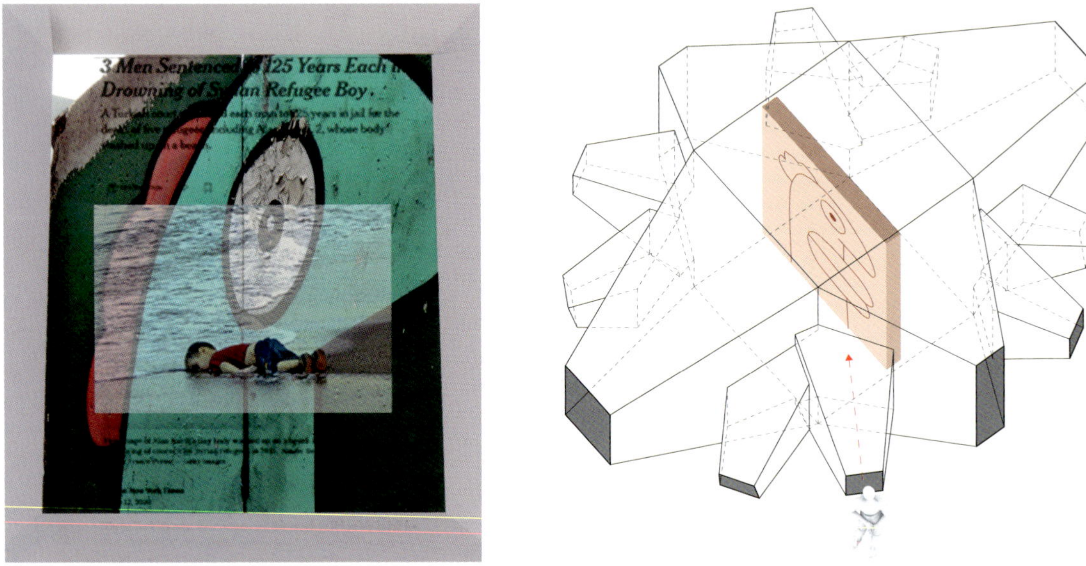

3.31 Berlin Wall in isocentric frame of reference. The image on the left shows the juxtaposition between the mural on the wall and the image located at the deictic axis.

In Figure 3.32 (bottom) we can see another juxtaposition: the lips of the mural framed over a news story of the tragedy. In this narrative, the bright red lips are motionless. The person reading this is reminded of the importance of her own voice. The mural reminds us that we have a responsibility to speak up and to act against atrocities. The person looking at these juxtapositions is encouraged to think of this segment of Berlin Wall not as a relic from the past, but as a reminder that human tragedies continue to unfold and peaceful coexistence of societies is contingent on fragile balances. These balances depend on perpetual emotional and cognitive empathy for each other, as much as they depend on international treatises and protocols.

3.32 Photographs of the physical model.

LOSING THE BALANCE IN THE P-SPACE, COGNITIVE DISSONANCE AND EMPATHY THROUGH GRIEF

In Herbert Clark's definition of P-space, a person stands upright on a ground plane, defined as the reference plane. Gravity is the only force that anchors a person to this reference plane, and it defines the directions of [above] and [below]. Clark's P-space is conceived to be on terra firma, even though he does not explicitly state it. Imagine defining the P-space at sea on a nautical vessel. The gravity that defines the vertical axis is now coupled by another force: buoyancy. The forces of buoyancy and gravity perfectly align on the same axis only when a ship floats in perfect trim. At this moment of perfect trim, a person standing on the naval vessel will be in a P-space where the horizontal plane acts, in theory, as the ground plane, but it is fundamentally different.

Even in dead flat water, the perfect trim creates a horizontal plane for a person to stand upright only temporarily. Because, unlike the reference plane on terra firma, on a ship the reference plane is a place of constant negotiations between the opposing forces of gravity and buoyancy. As the nautical vessel heels, the axes of gravity and buoyancy shift, and between these two parallel forces, a rotational correction is generated toward balancing the heel. Therefore, a person standing on this vessel experiences two reference planes: one is the physical tilted floor that is defined by the heel, and the second is the horizontal reference plane that is the plane of balance, which exists only temporarily.

The directions of our deictic center are in constant motion, and only on momentous occasions, with the alignment between the forces of gravity and buoyancy, do we catch the moment of perfect balance. Since our a priori understanding of P-space is naturally formed on land, the experience of P-space on a ship, due to the constant swing of the ground plane caused by these coupling forces, requires a translation of our L-space. If, as Clark argues, there is to be a strong relationship between the P-space and L-space, we can hypothesize that, a person who is born on a ship and has never set foot on land, until their complete acquisition of language, will have a much different L-space than a person born and raised on land. This person may develop a different conception of balance than their land born counterpart.

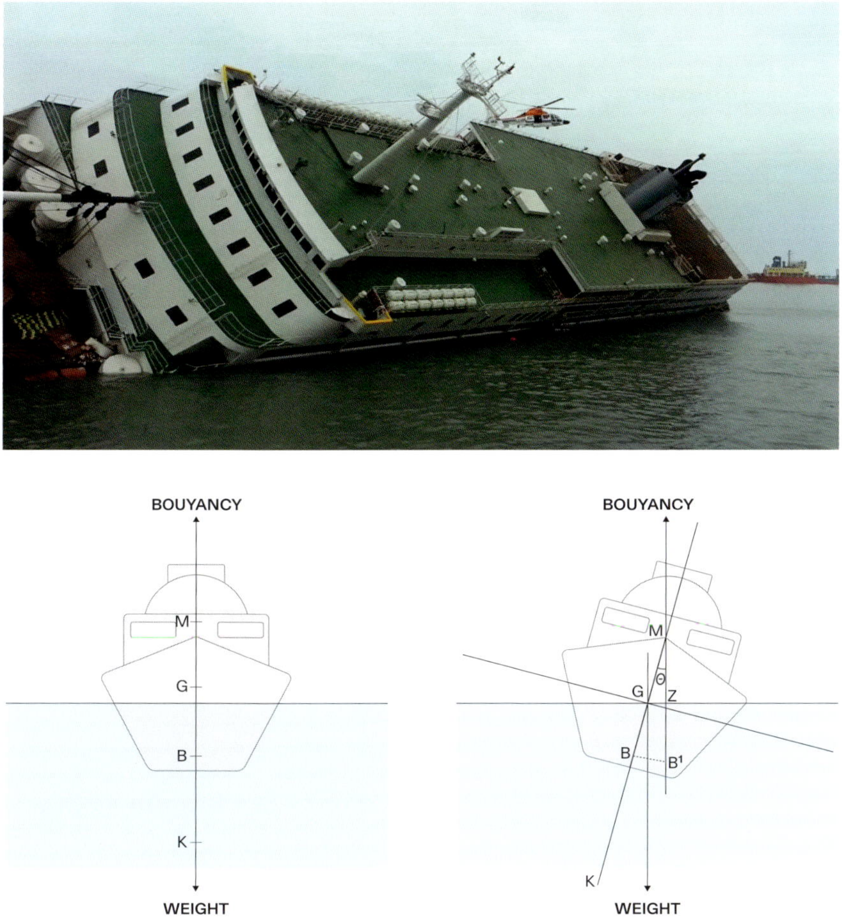

3.33 (Top) MV Sewol listing dangerously. (Below) Diagram showing the opposing forces of gravity and buoyancy.

The balance on a ship in some circumstances does not restore itself. The coupling forces between buoyancy and gravity are vectoral, and when they do not counter each other—in other words, when the axis of gravity shifts to form a negative moment arm—the tilt will increase, first gradually, then exponentially, as the moment arm increases, and the ship will eventually sink. The vectoral misalignment can be the slightest of angles that initiates a trajectory of no return, and with that, the reference plane (what we associate with the horizontal ground plane) in our P-space, and hence our understanding of balance, is irrecoverable.

On April 16, 2014, 2.7 kilometers off the coast of Byeongpungdo Island on the southern tip of South Korea, a naval tragedy took place. The MV Sewol ferry made a sharp turn, causing it to list 20 degrees into the water, which in turn caused its cargo to move on one side of the ship, tilting the ship further and effectively losing its restoring force. The shift of the cargo and the heel angle of the ship resulted in a negative righting moment, which initiated an irreversible process. In approximately two and a half hours, the ship sunk, and with it 306 people died. Of the victims, 250 were students from Danwon High School who were on a school trip.

When the MV Sewol made its fatal turn, it initiated the irreversible course of events governed by the rules of hydrostatics. At that moment something else was initiated as well: the P-space inside the ship altered. The upright position of our land born P-space was now stuck on an angle that could not restore itself. When we are in the sea born P-space, we are in a translation mode, like someone in a foreign country who is constantly translating. The meaning of being upright means being in balance, or, as Clark states, in our "canonical position." Our L-space—which encompasses our understanding of the world—has been defined by this canonical position.

What happens if the balance between the forces of buoyancy and gravity is lost, and the heel does not correct back to the horizontal plane? What does one feel in a P-space of gradual loss of balance? According to social psychologist Leon Festinger, a disequilibrium or a cognitive dissonance is an uncomfortable internal state that we need to resolve.[37] For instance, when it rains and we don't get wet, we would be in a state of dissonance, because this condition would be contrary to all our past experiences.[38] Likewise, we expect the forces of buoyancy and gravity to continuously balance themselves out in a ship so that we know that we are safe. For our land-based L-space, this means that we can still find our canonical position on a reference plane that mimics the ground even if it does it momentarily between the swings of the coupling forces.

On a ship, a tilt that is not restoring itself is an unfamiliar and scary territory to be in. The impact of the tilt inside the MV Sewol is heard in the emotional video recordings of the students trapped on board. They laughed in the beginning, even joking whether this event might make it to the evening news.

They mentioned the Titanic, the infamous naval disaster of modern times. In these online recordings, you could hear them sing the song from the feature movie. But as time passed in their disconcerting condition, they observed the increasing angle of the tilt. They propped themselves on the walls so as not to slide. One student, who was getting increasingly upset looking at the tilt, can be heard saying:

> "The ship is 85 degrees tilted, the temperature in my brain 100 degrees."
>
> "Do you see? The ferry is being sunk. Being sunk…"[39]

Their laughs and jokes gradually turn into farewell messages to their parents. They plead to be rescued. They didn't want to die. They were scared.

In February 2021, the City of Ansan, where the Danwon High School is located, announced an international design competition for a memorial park and building. The competition brief identified three design objectives for the project: first, to create "a space of remembrance and respect for life," where the memory of this tragic event is remembered through education programs and exhibitions; second, to create "a space for recognition and raising issues," such as the poor judgement of the captain and the crew, the incompetencies of the rescue effort during the disaster, and the State authorities' dismal response during and after the disaster that led to a national upheaval.[40] The organizers of the competition wanted to make this project a forum to discuss the State's responsibility "in face of social disasters." The third design objective was to create "a space for mourning and commemoration." As such that, "the memorial park shall go beyond the modern concept of seeing life and death as two completely separate things. Rather, it shall connect and remember death with present life."[41]

To design an architectural proposal that tries to fulfill these three objectives is both an ambitious and emotional undertaking. My firm worked on this design competition in the midst of the Covid pandemic, as we were all scattered away from our studio and connecting only virtually. After reading more about the disaster and watching the online posts of the students, we decided to come back to the studio. The grief we felt was too deep to bear

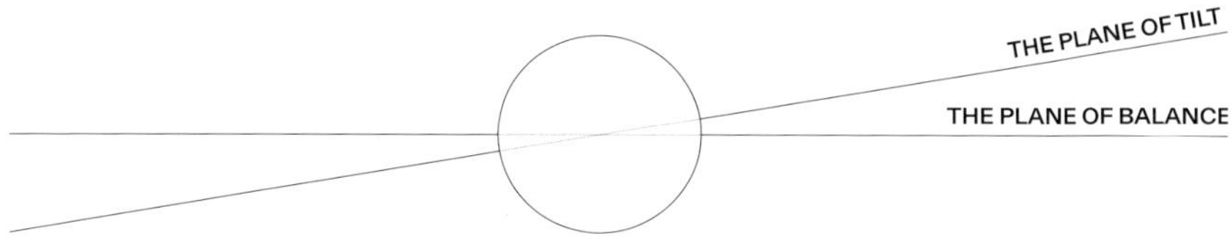

3.34 Concept diagram of the proposal, showing the plane of tilt and plane of balance.

alone. As we were all feeling our own fragility in this seemingly foreign land created by the pandemic, we tried to "feel into" how it felt for those on the ship, where the balance first gradually and then, irrecoverably, was lost.

It was this questioning that led us to the concept of our proposal: to create a space of negotiation between the tilt and the upright. By challenging the land-born understanding of our P-space, the design intent is to create a new L-space that can help us develop empathy with what it means to be in a place where the balance between buoyancy and gravity is forever lost.

The project creates an oblique volume that intersects the ground, shaping two major planes: the plane of tilt and the plane of balance. The tilted plane defines the floor of the building, as such it becomes the new ground plane. Whereas the horizontal plane, which relates to our land-born canonical position and represents what balance means to us, exists in the project as a juxtaposition of the plane of tilt to remind visitors that they are inside a new P-space. The tilt of the building causes it to sink into the ground plane on one end, which is defined by a reflecting pool, and on the other end it cantilevers over it. The enshrinement space is located below the reflecting pool.

The two planes intersect at the center of the Memorial, which is marked by a cylindrical space—the Hall of Harmony. (Figure 3.35) In this space, the datum line of balance is marked by a horizontal slit opening, which is connected to the reflecting pool outside. Water gently sips into the Hall of Harmony from the port side of the space, referencing the port side tilt of the ferry. The upright exists only in the center, and visitors explore moving toward the port side that is wet or the starboard side of the hall that is dry. As visitors swing inside this space, they experience the changing notions of the P-space—constructing for themselves the meaning of balance and its loss.

3.35 Hall of Harmony

They are reminded that the ground plane is not to be taken for granted.

As the building cantilevers out over the reflecting pool, the sloping plane of the exhibition hall visually connects through an upside-down oculus to the Enshrinement Space, located underneath the reflecting pool. The exhibition hall receives its light only from the reflected light beams that bounce off the pool. Visitors can feel the omnipresence of the Danwon High School students in this space, and they are reminded that the exhibited sneakers, sweaters, headphones that were salvaged from the ship are not mere everyday objects. They are extraordinary reminders of unfulfilled lives. There is a visceral connection between the physical objects that once belonged to the students and their omnipresence within the spaces. The upside-down oculus reverses the positive axis of our land-born P-space. [Below] becomes [above].

The premise of our design proposal for the memorial park and building is to create dissonance, by altering the P-space of the visitor, changing their canonical position, so that as they search for equilibrium, they will need to challenge the meaning of balance. From the perspective of educational psychology, cognitive dissonance is central to knowledge development.[42]

3.36 Diagram showing the juxtapositions of the plane of tilt, the plane of balance, and the upside-down oculus.

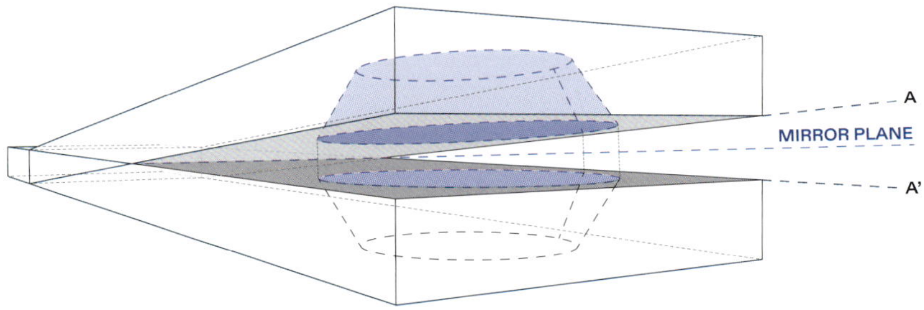

3.37 (Top) Interior rendering of the Exhibition Hall showing the upside-down oculus looking at the reflecting pool; (below) exterior view, looking at the upside-down oculus and the reflecting pool.

3.38 (Above) Section axonometric through the Enshrinement Space, Reflecting Pool and Exhibition Hall; (Below) 416 Memorial Park & Building view from the park that shows the tilting plane that cantilevers over the reflecting pool.

According to Piaget, perturbation or conflict is "the most influential factor in acquiring new knowledge structures."[43] In fact, he argues, it is only through continuous equilibration of disequilibria that we develop better cognitive constructs.

The cylindrical space of the Hall of Harmony, the oblique plane of the museum, and the upside-down oculus are all spatial constructs that challenge the established norms of our canonical position, and hence demand the visitor to create a new L-space, a new meaning of balance. The dissonance in space requires the visitor to continuously search for equilibrium, and thereby, as Piaget argued, allows the development of better cognitive constructs. In this process, the emotional empathy that develops out of our grief deepens into taking cognitive perspectives toward loss, remembrance, and our collective responsibilities in the face of social disasters.

SUMMARY: THE GEOMETRY OF EMPATHY

The interdisciplinary connections amongst discourses of spatial cognition, language acquisition, and development theory create an important basis to theorize the transformative potentials between perspectival projections in the physical (architectural) environment and perspective-taking in psychology.[44] Based on these interdisciplinary readings, this chapter discussed how the physical environment can influence the development of perspective-taking, and more specifically, how the purposeful design of spatial constructs can nudge us toward being more empathic.

Deixis is the most obvious way language and context relate to each other.[45] The decision to explore design concepts based on deixis and empathy sprung from Herbert Clark's argument that our perceptual space (P-space) influences our language space (L-space).[46] His theory that the properties in P-space can also be found in the properties of L-space led me to the premise that if we can alter the perceptual space purposefully, we can potentially create new narratives, ones that can encourage us to be more empathic.

Geometry is a common ground that deixis and architecture share. The concepts of projective geometry are not merely rules of representation, but a set of forces that are omnipresent in our imagination and spatial perception, and consequently instrumental in the development of social and spatial cognition. As Robin Evans stated: "What connects thinking to imagination, imagination to drawing, drawing to building, and buildings to our eyes is projection in one guise or another, or processes that we have chosen to model on projection."[47] The connections listed in Evans's argument are also the connections that are proposed in this book between perspective taking in development theory and experiencing spatial perspectives in architecture.

Through the use of projective geometry, we can create spatial nudges that can encourage perspective taking. And furthermore, we can curate specific trompe l'oeil constructs that have the ability to shift deictic center. The premise of this theory is explored in the three niches conjecture. Like the reciprocity of vision described by Michel Foucault in Velasquez's painting *Las Meninas*, the three niches conjecture creates juxtapositions of perspectives.[48] In this design conjecture, within the field of forced perspective, the egocentric nature of deictic center is challenged, and students are encouraged to take the perspective of the other.

The visual echo in this construct encourages cognitive reflections, which moves the first person away from the deictic center and enables her to look at the scene from outside, and hence shift the spatial frame of reference from an egocentric to an allocentric one. The premise of the three niches conjecture is to help develop an awareness of the other person during the acquisition of deictic words and expressions in early learning.

In a similar forced-perspective construct, the Lima Museum Expansion Project explores the idea of visual counterpoint to reciprocate the time deixis. In this project, the significance of time within the discussion of empathy is the correlation of time with identity. The present viewer looks at the historical museum built as a colonial cultural export with an identity bias. Using projections as a form of dialogue—not between the architectural expressions of the buildings but between different times—allows the occupant of the present time to leave behind any identity bias and build a more layered cultural understanding that connects [now] with [before] and toward the times [earlier than before].

The two design strategies—the visual echo of the three niches conjecture and the visual counterpoint of the Lima Museum Expansion—explores shifting the deictic center within the axial configuration of the forced perspective. In both strategies, the shift in time and person deixis is indexed to the first person. By contrast, in an isocentric spatial frame of reference, multiple perspectives are indexed to a non-human object. The Berlin Wall Enclosure project explores such a frame of reference, whereby, a piece of the wall is located at the center of an apparatus that facilitates isocentric projections. The multiple projections from a single object, toward another person's deictic center, create a pluralistic narrative of the object. This type of a perspectival construct allows for a multifaceted juxtaposition, and thus creates a heightened level of awareness-of-being.[49]

And what happens if we break the rules and create a space where there's disequilibrium? From Festinger's perspective the cognitive dissonance is uncomfortable and it needs to be resolved.[50] Whereas, according to Piaget, in the process of equilibration of disequilibria we develop better cognitive constructs.[51] The 416 Memorial Park Project deliberately creates spatial constructs of disequilibrium, challenging what Herbert Clark calls as our canonical position, which defines our deictic center.[52] The premise of these spatial constructs is that through the search for balance we change, and we develop a more meaningful relationship with loss.

The discussion on deixis and empathy brings us to the crossroads of linguistics, development theory, and architecture. The theoretical framework of this book—the geometry of empathy—and the design conjectures that sprung from it, have emerged from this intersection and the following two chapters depend on the framework set here.

DEIXIS AND EMPATHY
CHAPTER NOTES

1 David Wood, *How Children Think and Learn* (Blackwell Publishing, Second Edition, 1998), 129.

2 Stephen Levinson, *Pragmatics* (Cambridge University Press, 1983), 62.

3 Charles Fillmore refers to the three categories of person deixis as "speaker, addressee, and audience." Charles Fillmore, *Lectures on Deixis* (Stanford: CSLI Publications, Stanford University, 1997), 62.

4 Fillmore, *Lectures on Deixis*, 61.

5 Fillmore, *Lectures on Deixis*, 61.

6 Fillmore, *Lectures on Deixis*, 61.

7 Levinson, *Pragmatics*, 64.

8 Levinson, *Pragmatics*, 64.

9 Eve Clark and C. Sengul. "Strategies in the acquisition of deixis," *Journal of Child Language* 5, No. 3 (1978), 457–475.

10 Clark and Sengul. "Strategies in the acquisition of deixis," 458.

11 Clark and Sengul. "Strategies in the acquisition of deixis," 457.

12 Jean Piaget, *The Child's Conception of the World* (Routledge & Kegan Paul Ltd, 1971), 167.

13 Barbara Tversky, "Spatial Perspective in Descriptions" in *Language and Space*, eds. Bloom, Peterson, Nadel, and Garrett (The MIT Press, 1996), 463.

14 Michael J. Proulx et al., "Where Am I? Who Am I? The Relation Between Spatial Cognition, Social Cognition and Individual Differences in the Built Environment," *Frontiers in Psychology* 7 (February 11, 2016), 5. https://doi.org/10.3389/fpsyg.2016.00064.

15 Proulx et al., "Where Am I? Who Am I?," 5.

16 Proulx et al., "Where Am I? Who Am I?," 14.

17 Michel Denis, *Space and Spatial Cognition: A Multidisciplinary Perspective* (Routledge, 2018), 65.

18 Denis, *Space and Spatial Cognition*, 66.

19 Richard Thaler and Cass Sunstein, *Nudge: Improving Decisions About Health, Wealth and Happiness* (Penguin Books, 2008).

20 Tversky, "Spatial Perspective in Descriptions," 487.

21 Carol Garhart Mooney, *Theories of Childhood: An Introduction to Dewey, Montessori, Erikson, Piaget, and Vygotsky* (Redleaf Press, 2013), 82.

22 Herbert Clark, “Space, time, semantics and the child” in *Cognitive Development and the Acquisition of Language*, ed. T.E. Moore (Academic Press, 1973), 28.

23 Clark, “Space, time, semantics and the child,” 28.

24 Clark, “Space, time, semantics and the child,” 28.

25 Clark, “Space, time, semantics and the child,” 34.

26 Clark, “Space, time, semantics and the child,” 35.

27 Clark, “Space, time, semantics and the child,” 30.

28 The use of “perspectival hinge” in this context indicates a method of translation between the forms of representation and the world to which they refer. For more discussion on this, refer to: Alberto Pérez-Gómez and Louise Pelletier, *Architectural Representation and the Perspective Hinge* (The MIT Press, 1997).

29 Robin Evans, *The Projective Cast: Architecture and Its Three Geometries* (MIT Press, 1995), xxvi.

30 Evans, *The Projective Cast*, 369–70

31 Kenneth Frampton, *Le Corbusier* (Thames & Hudson, 2001), 182.

32 The Philips Pavilion form is generated through musical compositions of Xenakis and Corbusier’s Modular. For a broader discussion on this, refer to: Frampton, *Le Corbusier*, 182; or Evans, *The Projective Cast: Architecture and Its Three Geometries*, 298.

33 On the total work of art in Le Corbusier’s architecture refer to: Frampton, *Le Corbusier*.

34 Anthony McCall, *Line describing a cone*, film, 1973.

35 Anthony McCall, *Elements for a Retrospective, 1972–1979 / 2003*. Serpentine Gallery, London, 14.

36 Thierry Noir, “The Berlin Wall,” https://thierrynoir.com/biography/essays/berlin-wall/

37 Leon Festinger, *A Theory of Cognitive Dissonance* (Stanford University Press, 1957).

38 Festinger, *A Theory of Cognitive Dissonance*, 14.

39 “MV Sewol Ferry Disaster” YouTube, https://www.youtube.com/watch?v=BaXiEP-nYfs.

40 416 Memorial Park International Design Competition Design Guideline, The City of Ansan, 2021.

41 416 Memorial Park International Design Competition Design Guideline.

42 Amy Adcock, “Cognitive Dissonance in the Learning Processes” in *Encyclopedia for the Sciences of Learning* (Springer Press, 2012), 588.

43 Jean Piaget, *The Equilibration of Cognitive Structures: The Central Problem of Intellectual Development*. Translated by Terrance Brown & Kishore Julian Thampy (University of Chicago Press, 1985), 33.

44 Recognizing that connecting perspective taking with spatial (architectural) perspectives may be interpreted as a "cognitive shortcut" for an architect. Cognitive shortcuts are impactful in our decision making, and henceforth the design conjectures of this book may not have come to fruition without my architectural background. Even though, I have situated the thesis of the book through multi-disciplinary readings, "Architecture can change the world" the undercurrent of my cognitive bias cannot be understated in the formation of this key argument of the book.

45 Levinson, *Pragmatics*, 54.

46 Clark, "Space, time, semantics and the child"

47 Evans, *The Projective Cast*, xxxi.

48 Michel Foucault, *The Order of Things: An Archaeology of the Human Sciences* (Routledge, 1994), 4.

49 "Awareness-of-being" is used in reference to Heidegger's phenomenological analysis of existence or "being-in-the-world" (*in-der-Welt-sein*).

50 Festinger, *A Theory of Cognitive Dissonance*.

51 Piaget, *The Equilibration of Cognitive Structures*

52 Clark, "Space, time, semantics and the child," 35.

4

MOVEMENT AND EMPATHY

From spatial exploration to social learning

We move, even when we stand still. Our eyes blink, our hearts beat, our lungs contract and expand, our arms twitch, even in the most steady-state moment. Absolute stillness is not for the living. In early childhood, as Piaget's studies show, we associate life with movement.[1] Whether it is a bike that moves or a caterpillar that crawls, they are both equally alive for our young minds. Only at later stages of development do we learn to differentiate spontaneous movement from movement imposed by an outside agent, and associate life only with the former. In other words, we learn to differentiate the movement of the bicycle which is caused by the biker—an outside agent—from the movement of the caterpillar, which is intrinsic and created by itself.

Through movement we discover our bodies and develop our motor skills. We also develop an understanding of the environment by moving through it. Movement allows us to experience the world from multiple perspectives, expanding our egocentric view toward allocentric ones. From early childhood, when we start discovering ourselves and our surroundings, to later stages of development, when we build social, emotional, and cognitive relationships, movement plays a catalytic role. And it is through movement that we interact with others. We learn to socialize and develop skills that allow us to take perspectives other than our own. And by that, movement is key to empathy.

Buildings, on the other hand, are expected to stand still. When they move—if they shake in an earthquake or sway in the wind, for instance—we are terrified. The sense of stability of a building is taken for granted, but even in their assumed stillness, buildings never stop moving. Thermal movements cause materials to expand and contract, and floors deflect as they get subjected to occupant loads, like people coming in and out or as we roll heavy

4.1 (Facing page) Avenues Shenzhen Primary School climbing wall.

furniture onto them. But most of these movements are unnoticeable to the casual observer, and we only experience the traces that movement leaves behind, like cracks on the wall or the sound of a creaky floor.

The movement around buildings, however, is manifold and omnipresent. Spontaneous movements engulf buildings, like people entering and departing or birds nesting on the eaves, or the slow climb of ivy on their walls. There are also the imparted movements—movements imposed by outside agents, such as when we open a door—in and around the buildings that create constant activity. Buildings shape and are shaped by the movement within and around them.

During the design process of a building, the questions of movement often present themselves like a puzzle to be solved. How do we circulate a building? What are the functional relationships between the spaces that need to be connected? What are the required adjacencies? Such questions play a critical role in understanding, analyzing, and designing the programmatic requirements of a project. Some building typologies, like airports, rely on the successful resolution and delineation of different circulation networks, such as arriving passengers and departing ones; domestic versus international travelers; the taxi pick up line to public transportation network; taxiways of the planes and the ground transportation vehicles that share the same tarmac; or sorting out the different luggage paths and many other circulation networks associated with security and servicing.

However, circulation is not just a puzzle; our spatial perception is built on how we move through space. Movement allows us to see multiple perspectives, and see our environment from various vantage points, engaging our senses of vision, smell, hearing, and touch, as well as our sense of proprioception—the awareness of our body within space. Proprioception enables us to control the movements we make, but it also "provides us with the ability to perceive ourselves moving in space and acting in relation to our surrounding."[2] As we move within space, our awareness of being-in-the-world is indexed through the senses of our body, and therefore the interactions between body and space is key to the discussion on Movement and Empathy.[3]

HUMAN BODY

The relationship between architecture and the human body has a long history. As a form of shelter, architecture provides thermoregulation for the human body, protecting it from outside climatic conditions. Thinking of the building as a piece of clothing that wraps us or provides a second skin, as an extension of our bodies has played a significant role in architectural discourse. Indra Kagis McEwen, in her book on architectural beginnings, argues through etymological, literary, and visual references that there are multiple parallels between weaving and designing buildings and town planning.[4] They share the same desire to create order.

The other strand in the relationship of architecture and the human body is in the study of proportions. The fascination of anthropometric proportions of the human body historically has been discussed in metaphysical terms. In the first century BCE, the proportions of the human body were described by Vitruvius as the reference for designing "perfect buildings."[5] After outlining the proportions of the body parts, he presents a geometric depiction of the so-called "Vitruvian man":

> For if a man, be placed flat on his back, with his hands and feet extended, and a pair of compasses centered at his navel, the fingers, and toes of his two hands and feet will touch the circumference of a circle described therefrom. And just as the human body yields a circular outline, so too a square figure may be found from it. For if we measure the distance from the soles of the feet to the top of the head, and then apply that measure to the outstretched arms, the breadth will be found to be the same as the height, as in the case of plane surfaces which are perfectly square.[6]

The rediscovery of Vitruvius's writings in the fifteenth century played a key role in the art and architectural discourse of the Renaissance. In their conviction to create harmony in buildings through a system of mathematical ratios, Renaissance architects mirrored the proportions of the human body in their designs—a direct influence of Vitruvian thinking. The human body was seen as "the image of God" and "the proportions of his body are produced by divine will, so the proportions in architecture have to embrace and express the cosmic order."[7]

4.2 Leonardo da Vinci, *Vitruvian Man*, ca. 1492.

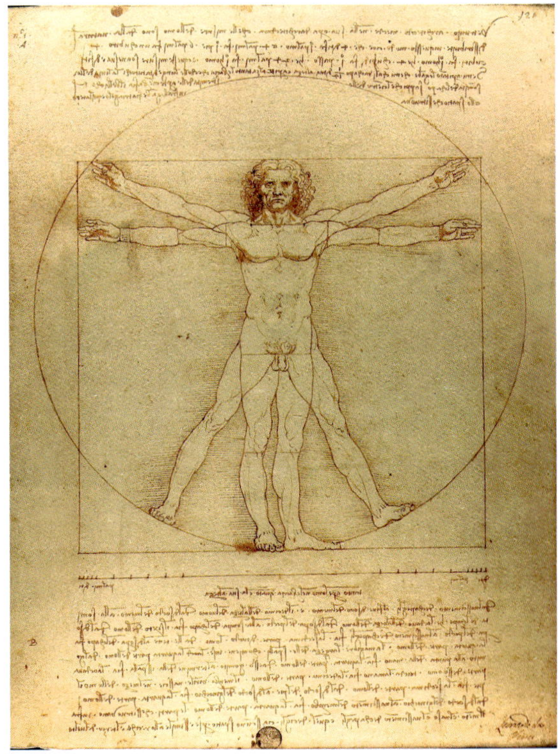

It is important to highlight that the emphasis on the ideal human figure is referenced as the adult Western male body. There is extensive critical writing about the emphasis on canonizing this body as the ideal human being. When considered from the perspective of human development, however, building a discourse on the adult body overlooks an array of relationships that develop throughout different stages of development.[8] We relate to the physical environment with our bodies, our perception of space is through our bodies, and at no time in human development is the relationship of the body and the physical environment more visceral than during early childhood.

Toddlers learn with their bodies. Putting objects into their mouths, banging on objects, tucking themselves into nooks and crannies are all part of their exploratory strategies, and an integral part of their developmental process. Insertion, especially, is a common spatial exploration strategy for this age

4.3 Toddlers learn with their bodies, and insertion is a spatial exploration strategy.

group. For instance, "when infants and toddlers learn to isolate one finger without extending the others, they begin to explore by insertion. They explore objects by putting fingers in objects or running fingers along their outside edges. As children explore, they also insert other body parts (hands, feet, legs, head, etc.) and their entire bodies into objects."[9] The spaces that allow for insertions of their bodies create a fun learning environment for toddlers.

For a movement room we designed for the Avenues New York Campus Early Learning Center, we created a series of niches in different scales for the toddlers to explore. For instance, the egg-shaped niche in Figure **4.3** allows children to learn to stretch and balance their body using the curvature of the niche. The form of the niche suggests curling into a fetal position, and children are observed playing inside the niche, profiling their bodies in different forms against the curvature of the space.

4.5 Avenues New York Small World movement room.

The niches are scaled for the size of toddlers, allowing them to easily reach the walls of the eggs with their arms and legs. This stretching inside the niche is also observed in the playroom.[10] Toddlers stand up inside the niches and stretch their legs and arms, as they learn to balance and coordinate their movements. These spaces wrap their bodies and give them a sense of security and belonging. Not surprisingly, as observed by the teachers, the children refer to these eggs as "bedrooms."

The project has a larger niche to allow the children other exploratory activities. They use the netting to climb or balance their bodies while using foam rollers to coordinate their movements. The children also use this as a more social space to gather in groups. According to the teachers, the children like the sensory push and pull of the net.[11] They also like to observe through the net. The large egg niche is often referred by the children as the "elevator," which they call each other out to go inside as they run around the room. Given that the project is in New York City, where elevators are a ubiquitous part of urban life, this name choice is perhaps not surprising.[12] Elevators are confined spaces that are often occupied by multiple people. Their confined scale relative to other spaces is similar to the scale of the niches.

4.4 (Facing page) Learning to balance in the Avenues New York Small World egg niche.

4.6 Playscape study models.

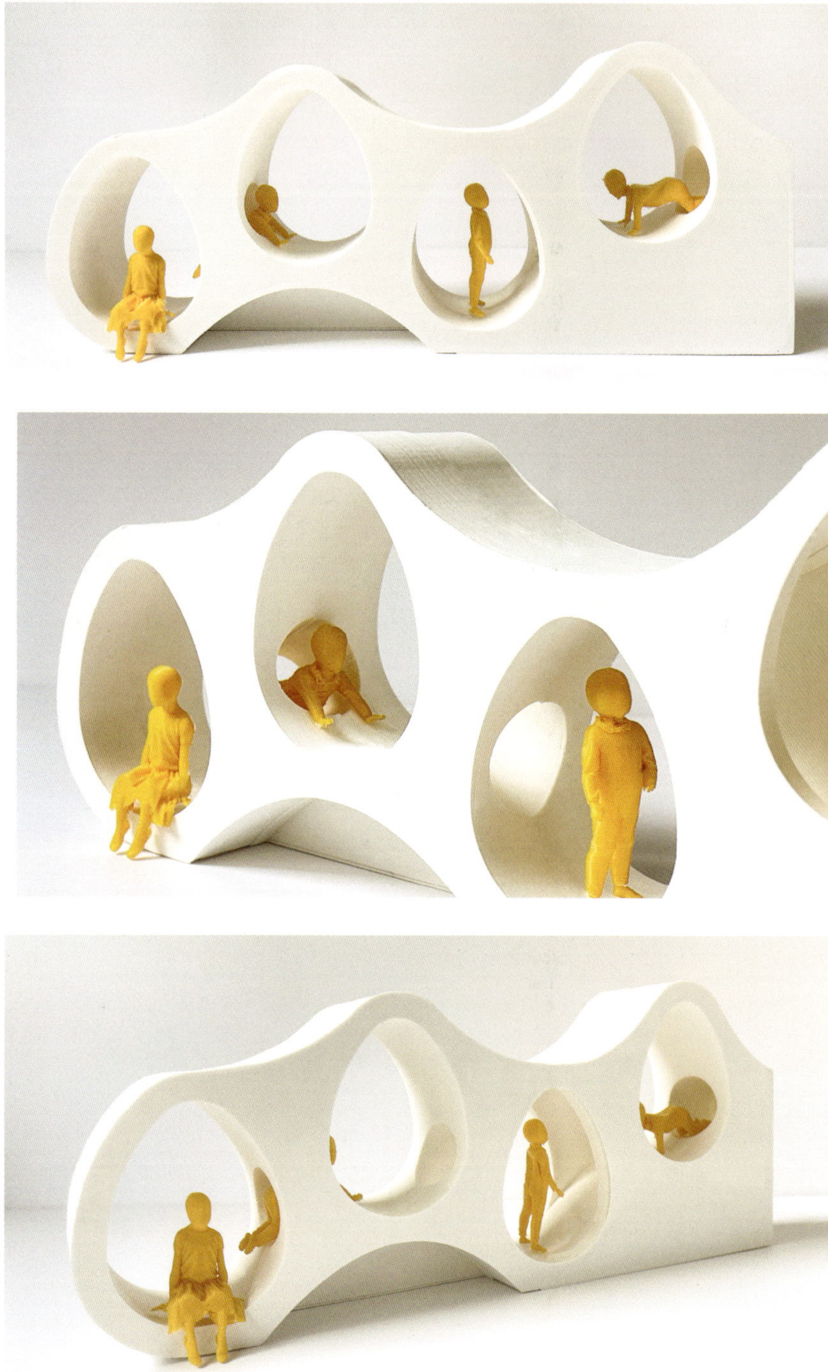

4.7 The sinuous forms of the playscapes encourage spatial exploration and help develop gross motor skills.

In a next version of this play structure, designed for another location, we added interconnections between different niches to create more intricate insertion areas for spatial exploration. In this version of the design, the connectivity between the egg niches creates a nested structure that allows the children to move from one niche to another through circular openings and slides. (Figure **4.6**) The profiling of the structures, where the children can move more actively, also plays an important role in their spatial explorations.

As seen in the insertion strategy, the relationship between the physical environment and the children's bodies is critical. For instance, concave and convex undulations in the playscapes offer multiple fun experiences. (Figure **4.7**) These forms help to exercise the movement of climbing up and down, and coordinate steps for the children. Upon many observations, children are seen rolling, sliding, and running over these forms, sometimes by themselves, sometimes playing with other friends. "Repetitive play is one of the ways in which children master major motor skills," and these undulating playscapes offer repetitions with variations.[13]

4.8 Children use the undulating playscapes to lay down and have slower pace play with each other.

The sinuous forms of the playscapes are designed to conform naturally to the human body, which helps children to engage the playscapes in multiple ways. For instance, we have observed that children lay down on the slopes, along the contours of the curves, and play with each other. The shapes allow them to engage in high-paced activities like running up and down, as well as pausing to lay down and play with each other more quietly. (Figure **4.8**) To ensure the curves of the playscapes were tuned to the body of young children, we conducted various studies on the sectional profiles of the contours. The scale, curvature, and syncopation of the concave and convex profiles were mapped out in full scale mockups and tested. This rigorous study was then translated to careful documentation of these profiles for fabrication of both the structural frames and soft upholstery coverings. (Figure **4.9**)

4.9 Fabrication photos of the playscapes (SiTu fabrication plant, Brooklyn, NY)

4.10 Avenues New York Small World Movement Room.

MOVEMENT AND SOCIAL LEARNING

Movement in early learning is an important part of physical, social, emotional, and cognitive development. According to Piaget's development theory, in the early stages of childhood, children start to develop their motor skills. They are discovering their bodies, moving their limbs around, trying to build coordination into their movements, and they use the physical environment around them to build those skills. Describing Piaget's sensorimotor stage, Carol G. Mooney writes:

> Since motor development is a significant learning task of the sensorimotor stage, one of the most important supports to cognitive development that infant/toddler teachers can establish is a safe and interesting environment. Babies need to push, pull, and manipulate objects. They need to crawl, climb, and pull up to standing positions without being physically at risk…they need to experiment with spatial relationships and learn through their bodies…[14]

4.11 Avenues Shenzhen Primary School climbing wall.

Movement is also a part of play time; it is the most improvisational part of learning, where children discover themselves and their surroundings through movement. Even though early childhood is the most egocentric period of human development, children learn to socialize through movement. They don't play team sports, as this is too young an age to impose on structured play, but they use their imagination to invent their own play, engage their friends, and mimic their motions.

Learning with the body continues in later stages of development, even at ages when children shift from imaginative play to organized sports. As seen in Figure 4.11, for instance, grade 3 students are learning to climb in this outdoor playground. The climbing wall in this project is centrally located in the school's campus, to create a focal point, where activities can be shared and learned.

Learning from a more "skilled other," as discussed by Vygotsky, is an important consideration for the project. Being in the presence of more capable others, can inspire us or guide us to expand our personal development. Vygostky calls this the Zone of Proximal Development, which is "the distance between the actual development level as determined by independent problem solving and the level of potential development as determined through problem solving under adult guidance or in collaboration with more capable peers."[15]

The spatial configuration of the climbing wall and its central location on campus are instrumental in creating an environment for the Zone of Proximal Development. The pleated climbing wall is adjacent to a covered playground, and it is nested within a space that is open to the sky. The sectional height difference between the covered playground and the climbing wall creates a dramatic light effect—the natural light washes down the wall, creating an uplifting sense in the space. Facing this area are the student commons and the dining hall. This adjacency to the main assembly spaces on the campus puts a further focus on the climbing wall. It energizes the campus and celebrates social learning through movement.

The backdrop of the shared joy of climbing by these students is noteworthy to underline, as this is the premise of the thesis presented here: architecture can play a significant role in how we learn.

ARCHITECTURE OF CONNECTIONS

A much-discussed topic in school planning is how circulation is managed during student drop-off and pick-up as these are the peak times for movement into and around campus. Depending on the urban context, vehicular traffic gets layered into these discussions. Are students coming by bus? Are they dropped off by their parents? Is there enough queuing space for the cars? While these questions are all part of the circulation puzzle that needs to be solved, they do not describe the critical role of circulation within learning environments themselves. Peak-time traffic brings a challenge of volume, but it does not reflect the intricacy of movement patterns that occur during the school day. As illustrated in the pedestrian flow study in Figure **4.12**, arrival time shows a simple, linear pattern of getting students from the point of entry to their learning spaces quickly and safely. By contrast, movement patterns during the school day—when students move between different classrooms,

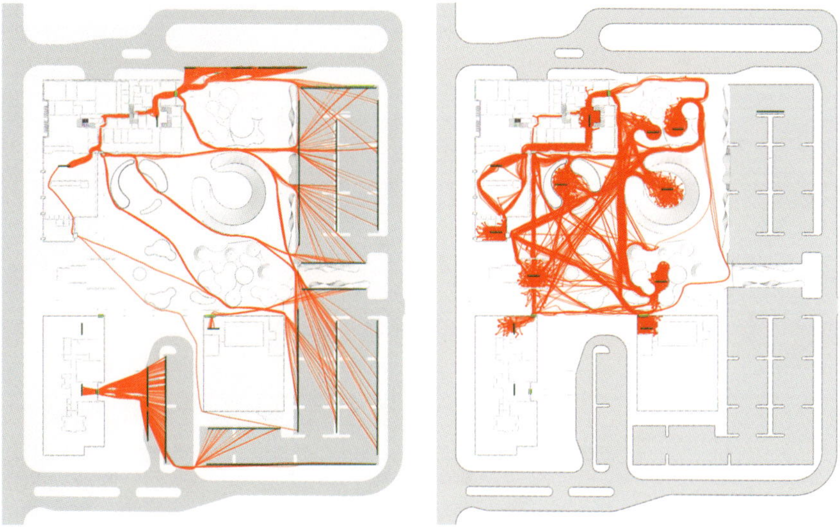

4.12 Pedestrian flow diagrams for a K-12 campus by Efficiency Lab for Architecture. The image on the left shows pedestrian flow at drop-off time. The image on the right shows the pedestrian flow during the school day. The pedestrian networks illustrated on the right shows a much more intricate and complex pattern of flow compared to the one on the left.

labs, commons, dining halls, athletic facilities, and outdoor spaces—appear as a much more complex network of circulation lines with clear nodes of denser activity.

The experience of movement through the school plays an important role in the quality of the learning environment. Movement is integral to students' spatial perception, and its careful choreography is, therefore, critical in fostering social interactions, encouraging explorations, and allowing for moments of drift.

In the late 1950s, the Situationist International, a movement formed by artists and political theorists, advocated for the concept of dérive (drifting) as a way to wander through cities unencumbered by the bias of movements governed by our daily routines. Theorized by Guy Debord, dérive through the urban environment is informed by "pyschogeographic" attractors.[16]
As Debord explained,

> [psychogeography] attempted to combine subjective and objective modes of study. On the one hand it recognized that the self cannot be divorced from the urban environment; on the other hand, it had

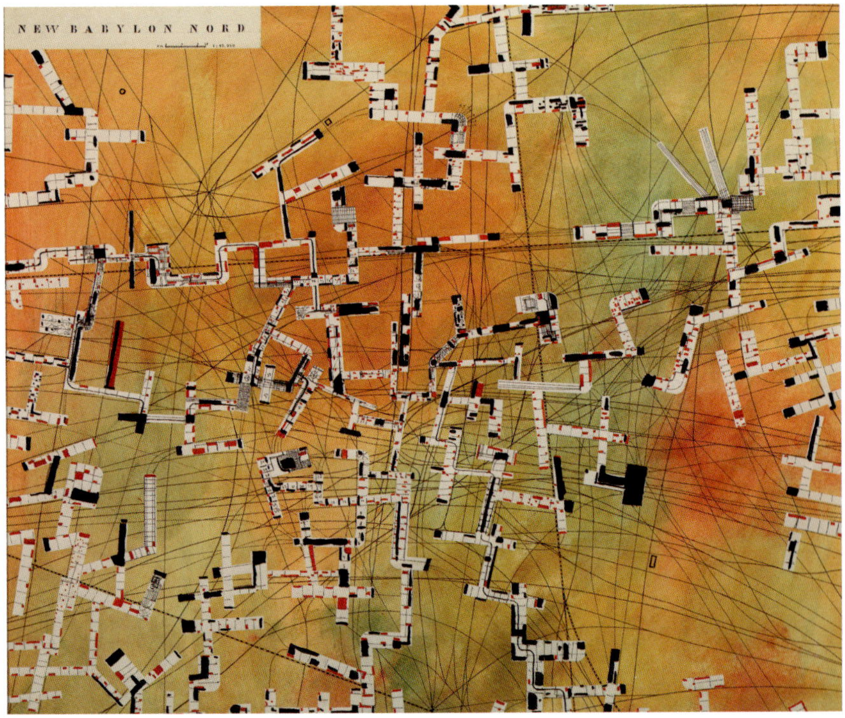

4.13 Constant, North New Babylon, 1959, watercolor on collage, Kunstmuseum Den Haag.

> to pertain to more than just the psyche of the individual if it was to be useful in the collective rethinking of the city.[17]

Dérive was not simply a past time activity of strolling, but it was a "playful, constructive behavior" characterized with spontaneity and chance.[18]

The Situationist theory of dérive was manifested in the work of the Dutch artist Constant Nieuwenhuys (frequently referred to only by his first name) and his utopian city The New Babylon. Constant's city came to life in collages, large-scale models, and photo montages that included images of the models, superimposed with drawings and paintings. The fluidity of the spaces that interconnected at multiple levels, utilizing transformable structures, created spatial complexity for new experiences. This fascinating utopian city celebrated the labyrinthine movements of drifting, designed to foster creativity of the individual as well as the communal interactions of society.

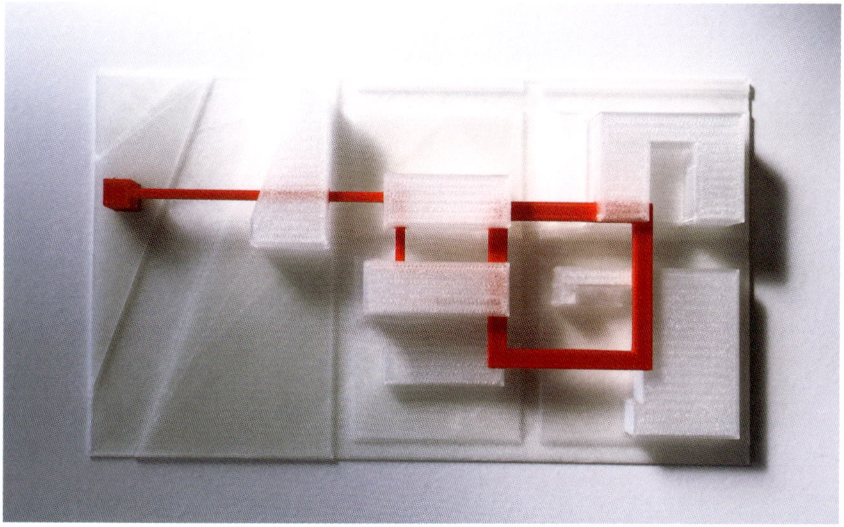

4.14 The red elements in the model represent connections between the buildings. Note the far-left connection that extends across the street to a public park to integrate the campus with the larger neighborhood context. The red square forms the sky quad.

4.15 (Following spread) Sky quad connecting multiple buildings on campus. The Sky quad bridge weaves through buildings, hovers over terraces and courtyards to create a well-defined heart of the campus.

Inspired by the idea of drift, we designed a network of connections for an urban campus in Shenzhen that celebrates the improvisational quality of explorations while allowing for different scales of social gathering. The multiple buildings on campus, which are spread around a dense urban neighborhood, are connected by a network of elevated connections, weaving the campus together. As seen in the model photos (Figure **4.14**), the red connection network that floats over the city grid establishes a sense of community within the campus that is unencumbered by the vehicular traffic. The campus circulation network is juxtaposed over the urban fabric, providing layers of connection to the streets and the adjacent public park, to create a fluid engagement with the community, and thereby situating the school in its context.

The epicenter of this connective network is the "sky quad," which is the heart of the campus. The circulation between buildings defines a three-dimensional matrix of spaces that allows both a sense of communal gathering and small group break-out spaces. The labyrinthine spatial qualities of the sky quad help promote discovery and exploration. As in the vision of Constant's New Babylon, the boundaries are eroded, and the spaces flow one into another, promoting drift.

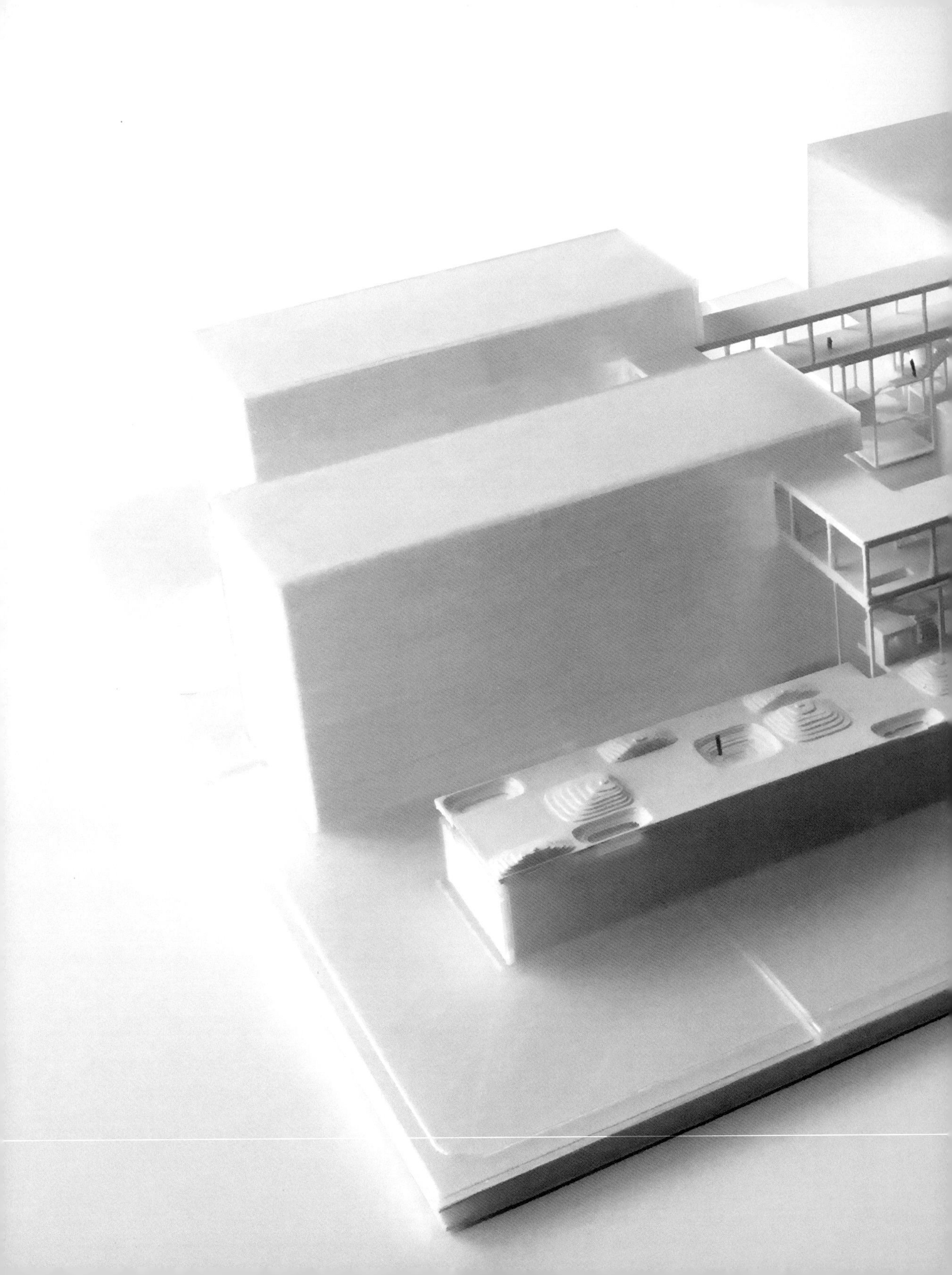

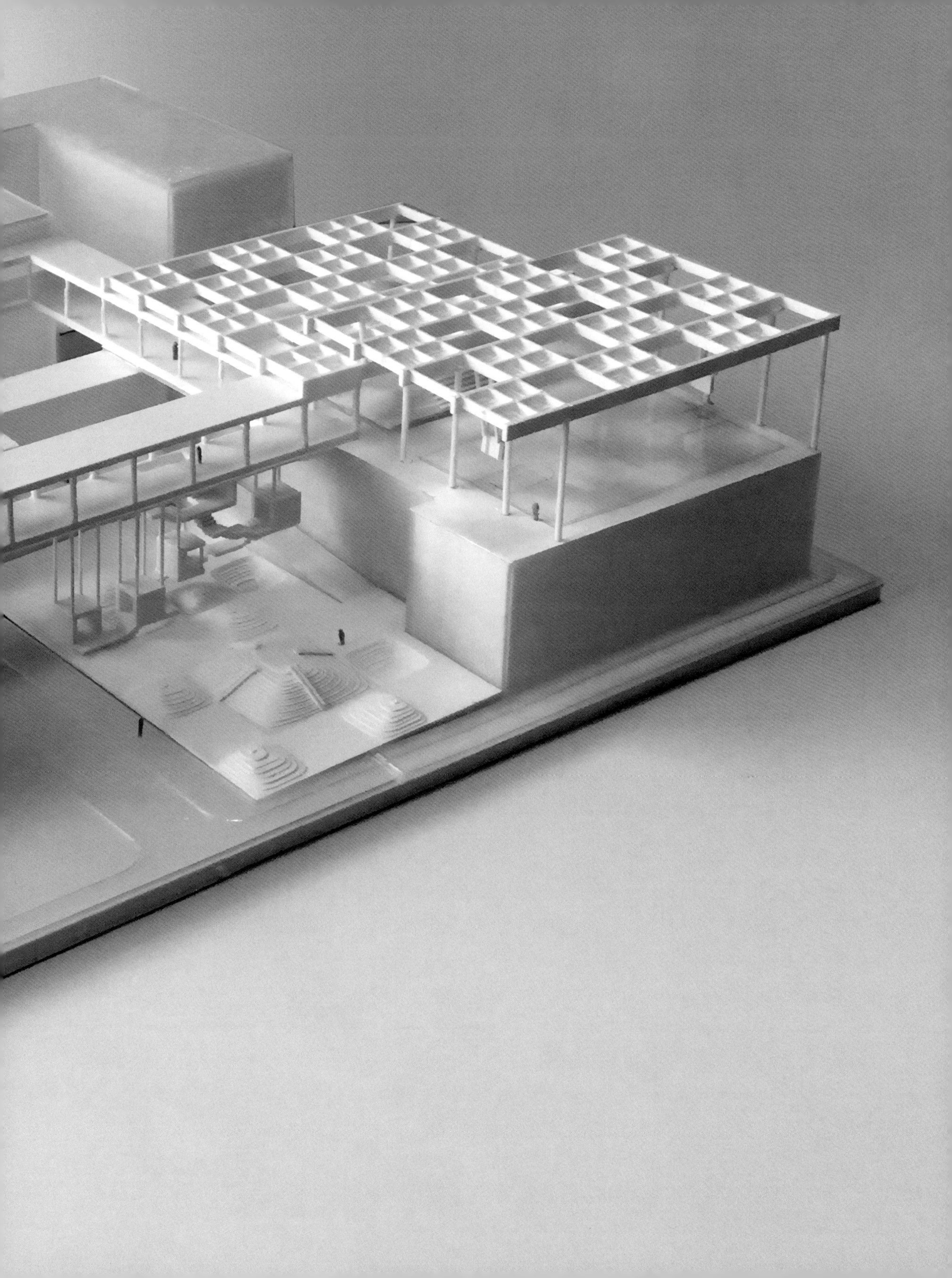

PEDESTRIAN MOVEMENT

To expand the discussion on movement, it is beneficial to understand the science of pedestrian flow—a discipline that traditionally falls in the realm of traffic engineers and movement planners. Over the last fifty years, the studies to understand and model pedestrian flow are manifold, ranging from empirical studies based on field observations to analytical theories that are influenced by a variety of disciplines ranging from fluid dynamics to psychology. For instance, the Social Force Model for pedestrian dynamics, developed in 1990s and which set the basis for an array of pedestrian simulation models, is influenced by the work of psychologist Kurt Lewin.[19] On the other hand, grid-based movement modeling has its roots in cellular automata—discrete (finite) computational systems often used to represent non-linear dynamics.

In the early 1970s, John J. Fruin, an engineer working for the Port Authority of New York & New Jersey, researched the bi-directional movement of crowds by using timelapse photography in the transportation hubs of New York City. His seminal work, "Designing for Pedestrians: A Level-of-Service Concept," defined what is now widely established as the Fruin index of level of service (LOS) for pedestrian flow. Fruin's study built a framework to "provide a qualitative method of designing new or evaluating existing pedestrian environments."[20] Studying different pedestrian densities on walkways and stairways, Fruin developed his levels of service, and defined in each one of them the speed and quality of walking, potential conflicts with other pedestrians, and the functional appropriateness of them. For instance, Level-of-Service-A (LOS-A) for walkways is defined as,

> Equivalent to an average pedestrian area occupancy of 35 sq ft per person or greater, at level of service a sufficient area is provided for pedestrians to select freely their own walking speed, to bypass slower pedestrians, and to avoid crossing conflicts with others. Design volumes would be approximately 7 pedestrians per minute per foot width of walkway or less. Designs consistent with this level of service would include public buildings or plazas without severe peaking characteristics or space restrictions.[21]

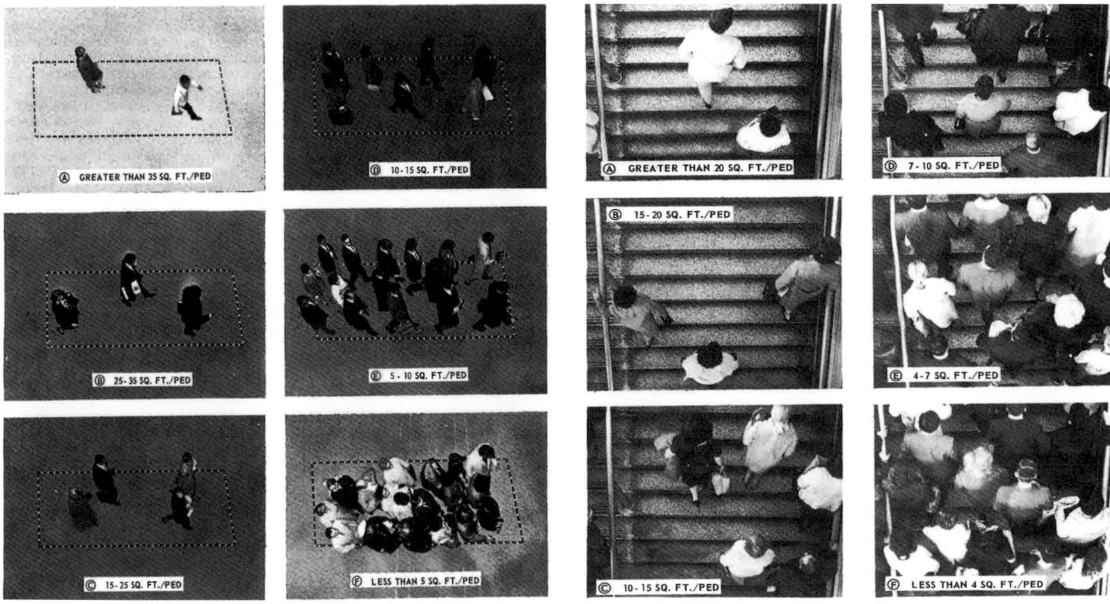

4.16 John Fruin, Level of Services. Diagrams illustrating the letter-coded system changing from Level A to F for (left) walkways and (right) stairways. Originally published in John J. Fruin, "Designing for Pedestrians: A Level-of-Service Concept."

Compare this level of service to LOS-F for walkways, defined as:

> Equivalent to an average area occupancy of 5 sq ft or less per person, at level of service F all pedestrian walking speeds are extremely restricted, and forward progress can only be made by shuffling. There would be frequent unavoidable contact with other pedestrians and reverse or crossing movements would be virtually impossible. Traffic flow would be sporadic with forward progress based on movement of those in-front. This level of service is representative of a loss of control and a complete breakdown in traffic flow. Pedestrian areas less than 5sq ft are more representative of a queuing than a traffic flow situation, and this level of service is not recommended for walkway design.[22]

Fifty years later, the Fruin index is still the benchmark guideline to define quality of services on walkways and stairways. In this book, the density evaluation results of agent-based computational pedestrian simulations are therefore reported in the Fruin LOS.

Fruin's employment with the Port Authority gave him the access and resources to observe one of the busiest transportation hubs in the world and compile real-world data points.

Data collection is a critical task in understanding movement. Unlike vehicular flow, however, where cars stay on roads and in their lanes, pedestrian flow is much more complicated and improvised, and hence it is harder to collect data. People don't stay in dedicated paths and there are not many restrictions that inhibit free movement. People also use three-dimensional paths like stairs, ramps, and elevators, which makes visual mapping more challenging. To collect data in real life conditions, manual counting, timelapse photography, video imaging, sensors (microwave radar, pressure), detectors (laser, ultrasonic), and mobile device tracking technologies are utilized with varying levels of success. Some of these are harder to implement in complex spatial settings to have valuable reading.

To understand isolated incidences such as bottle necks, cross traffic, or turning walkways with blind corners, the Institute for Advanced Simulation at Forschungszentrum Jülich in Germany conducts lab-controlled experiments.[23] Overhead videos record these experiments, and the data generated through each of these scenarios are shared in open platforms to help build a better understanding of pedestrian behavior. Moreover, these experiments help calibrate and build the correlating computer simulations. For instance, the research project on pedestrian movement around 90-degree and 180-degree bends for stairs conducted by Steffen and Seyfried utilizes the experiments to help refine the computer simulations.[24]

DEVELOPMENT OF PEDESTRIAN SIMULATION

Pedestrian flow analysis started in the domain of traffic engineers and movement planners. Not surprisingly, the early development of pedestrian simulation platforms was derived from vehicular simulation models. As Gregory Hoy points out, these early models "neglected the impact of interactions between pedestrians."[25] Other models used fluid dynamics to model the macro behavior of pedestrian flow. Borrowed from the equations of gas kinetics, these models illustrated some of the macro pattern formations that are observed in pedestrian flow. Dirk Helbing's research using complex fluid-dynamic equations to analyze pedestrian behavior illustrates examples of behavior patterns in scenarios such as dance floors and walking lanes.[26]

In the early 1990s, another approach to pedestrian simulation was developed by using Cellular Automata theory. The movement space is divided into a cellular grid and each cell accommodates a pedestrian or it is left empty. At each simulation time step, the pedestrian moves to the adjacent cell or stays in their cell. The transitions between cells are probabilistic.

In the 1990s, another approach was developed based on the Social Force Model. Kurt Lewin argued that behavioral changes are driven by social forces, stimuli that cause humans to divert from usual patterns.[27] This same theory has been applied to study and map pedestrian behavior. Helbing and Molnar, in their essay on Social Force Model for pedestrian dynamics, write:

> It is suggested that the motion of pedestrians can be described as if they would be subject to "social forces." These "forces" are not directly exerted by the pedestrians' personal environment, but they are a measure for the internal motivations of the individuals to perform certain actions (movements)....Computer simulations of crowds of interacting pedestrians show that the social force model is capable of describing the self-organization of several observed collective effects of pedestrian behavior very realistically.[28]

The Social Force Model describes the motion of users and specifically considers the availability of space in terms of proximity to other users and density of floor area, as well as direction of travel. Crowds of people and physical obstacles act as external "social force" stimuli that affect the path of travel.

The Social Force Model is formulated based on the following parameters.

- Desire Paths: The pedestrian desires to reach its destination as comfortable as possible, so they move in the shortest path without any detours at a comfortable speed.
- Repulsive Effects: This can be triggered by other pedestrians in the model

or by boundary conditions. The pedestrian does not want to get too close to other pedestrians in the model, keeping their territorial space. A stranger in the model can be repulsive to the other pedestrian. The boundary conditions in the model, like walls, act also as repulsive elements, as getting too close may be harmful.
- Attractive Effects: The pedestrian may be drawn to other people in the model, or they may come across attractions, like a storefront.

THE USE OF PEDESTRIAN SIMULATION IN THE DESIGN OF LEARNING ENVIRONMENTS

The pedestrian simulation examples included in this book are generated using Massmotion, an agent-based software tool, which uses the Social Force Model.[29] Key aspects of the software include:[30]

- Agents: These are the individual people in the simulation. The agents enter and exit the simulation through specified portals.
- Agent Attributes: These are the physical and behavioral attributes of the agent, such as walking speed, directional biases, or reactions to attractors that define how the agent interacts within the simulation environment.
- Agent Route Selection: The route selection of each agent can be specified either by defining multiple exit portals and letting the agent decide their own exit portal, or by predetermining the exit portal for the agent. In both scenarios, agents will take the "easiest" route possible.
- Agent Movement: The movement of agents is determined by a social forces algorithm calibrated in accordance with Fruin's Level of Service.

Considering that the evolution of pedestrian movement analysis has been focused on crowds—particularly in transit hubs, airports, large arenas, or in egress simulations—the choice of using these tools in learning environments may sound irrelevant. However, these simulations offer valuable insights ranging from large-scale campus master planning to understanding internal flow of the student commons. Some of our findings were, as expected, used to understand and manage density in bottleneck spaces and at peak times of movement. For instance, during drop-off and pick-up times, schools face similar pragmatic issues of crowd management, with which these simulations are designed to assist.

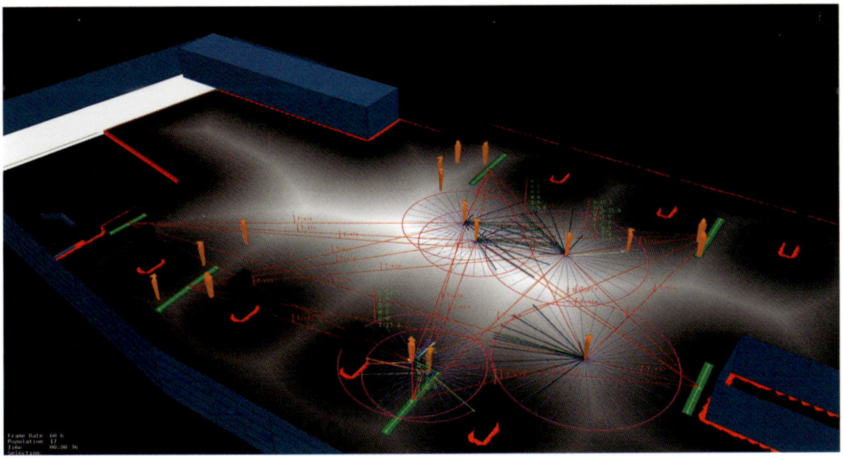

4.17 Screenshot of Oasys Massmotion pedestrian simulation analysis, which uses the framework of Social Forces Model.

The model illustrates the agents, the paths of travel, the obstructions, and attractions along the way.

The desire path parameter of the Social Force Model also proved a helpful tool in large-scale campus master planning. We have seen other examples of leveraging pedestrian simulations to assist in the design of public spaces by urban planners.[31] In similar vein, we have conducted large-scale simulations and designed campus frameworks that are informed by desire paths. As we explored deeper analysis at different scales, and by further leveraging the parameters of the Social Force Model, we found feedback loops between the agent behavior and the development concepts that we are exploring. For instance, the attractive and repulsive effects of agents toward other agents within the simulation help simulate scenes in assembly areas like commons or dining halls. These emulate what Dr. Julia Higdon highlighted in the Social Identity and Social Categorization Theory. (Refer to page 53)

To understand in-group and out-group dynamics, we conducted "cafeteria scene" simulations by tuning into these parameters to help design one of the most socially complex environments in schools. In addition, some of the sub-tools of the simulations that are designed for wayfinding, like the ability to map the gaze of the agents on vertical surfaces, proved to be a strong design tool. The visceral relationship between moving and seeing, and the ability to map them simultaneously in Massmotion inspired us to retool our design process and helped us design interconnected Student Commons.

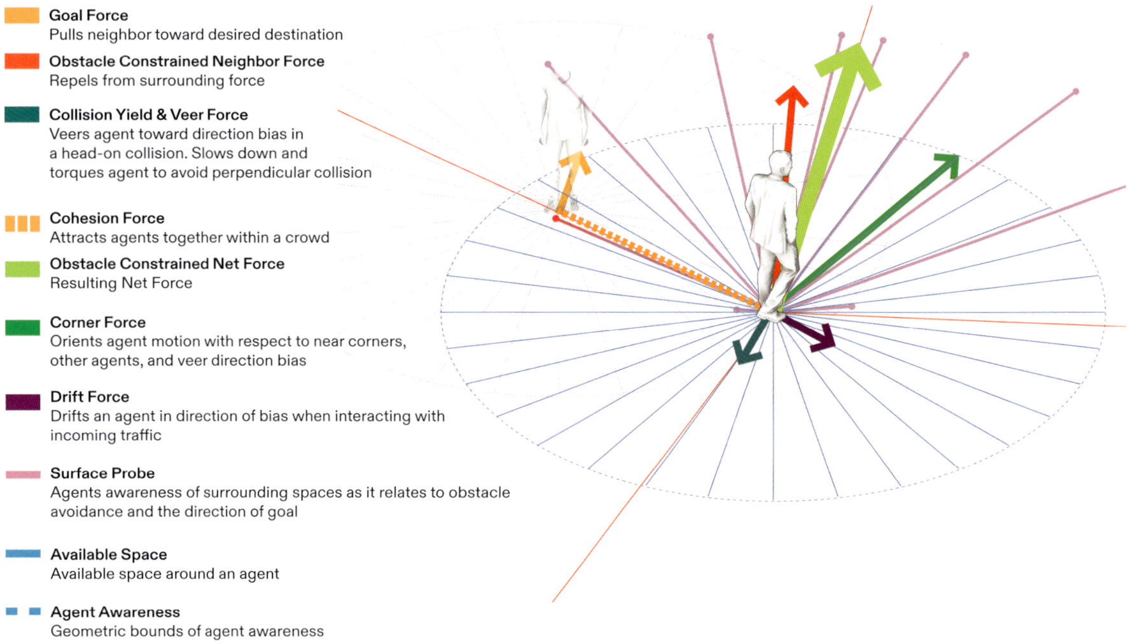

4.18 Diagram showing the social forces impacting the agent in the simulation.

We also tried to expand the simulation from its core premise of getting the agents out of the simulation with the shortest path possible, into keeping them in the simulation and letting them wander around. Our initial experiments with modeling labyrinths (Figure **4.19**) failed as the agents miraculously knew where the center of the labyrinth was and took the shortest path possible, without making any incorrect choices.

The Situationist International's theory of dérive did not apply to them. However, when we added attractors at each decision point of the labyrinth, it confused the agents from reaching the center in the shortest possible way. Some of the agents took the wrong turn toward the dead ends of the labyrinth, similar to what happens in real life conditions. In addition, when using attractors in the simulation, we saw patterns of wandering and exploration emerge. This led us to hypothesize that thoughtfully including psychogeographic attractors in the design of learning spaces will encourage beneficial drifting.

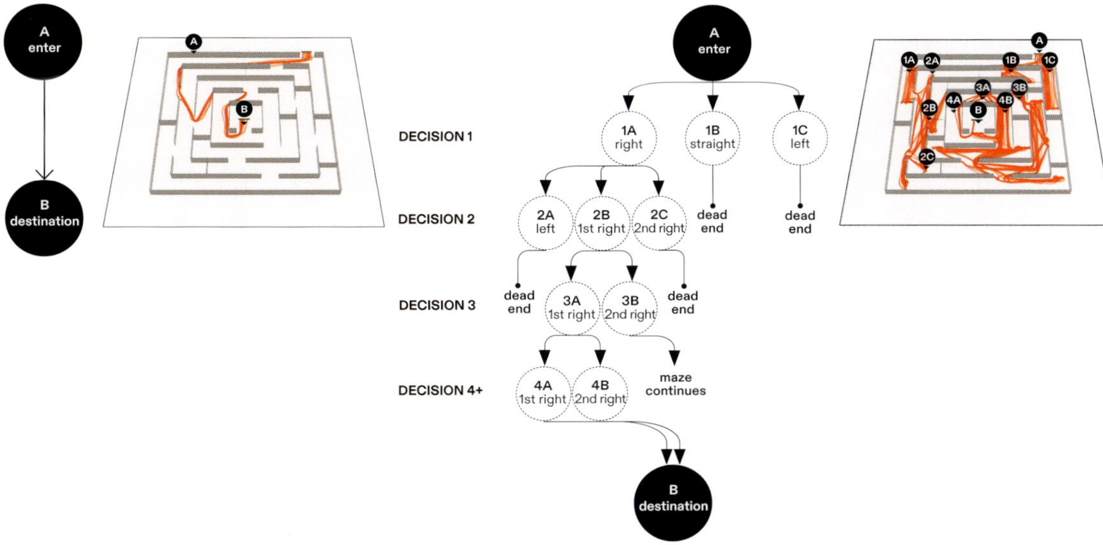

Like all experiments, there are varying levels of fulfillment in the following vignettes. Some of them, like the cafeteria scene, are unfulfilling yet provocative. They prompt critical discussions on how or whether the agent-behavior in computational simulations should be used to understand complex real life social issues.[32] On the other hand, the results of design experiments utilizing vision mapping simulations connect us back to discussions on deixis and empathy. Agents move in the perspectival space. The construct of the deictic center and the construct of the Social Force Model have similar attributes. (Figure **4.20**) Mapping the gaze of the agents on vertical surfaces allows us to understand the relationship between moving and seeing within the perspectival space, which also means we can evaluate the deictic contrast of the individual and the group.

4.19 Pedestrian simulation of labyrinth by Efficiency Lab for Architecture. The simulation is set with a single entry and exit portal. In the first iteration (left), the agents found the exit portal without making any mistakes. To wander around is not part of the software engine, and the agents need to be tricked (right) to deviate from the shortest path possible to the exit portal.

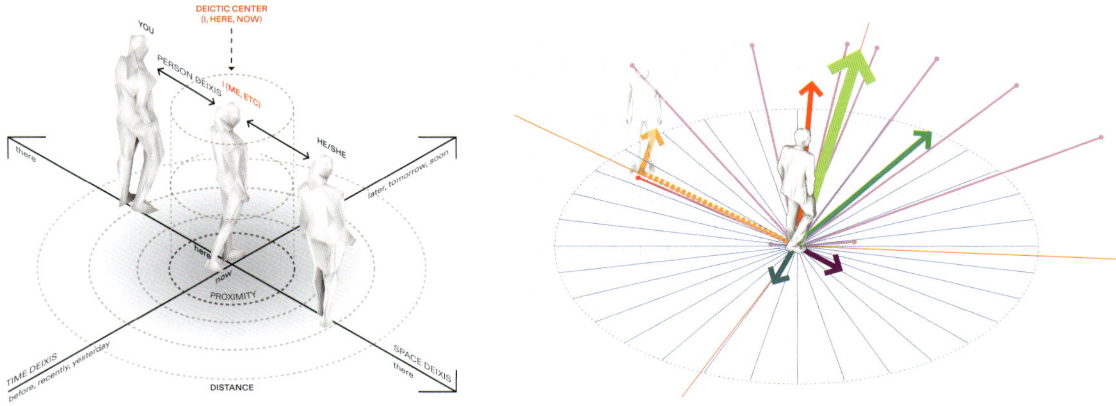

4.20 (Left) Deictic center; (right) Social Force Model in the pedestrian simulation analysis.

(A) Managing Density:

In 2020, the re-opening schools during the Covid pandemic posed manifold challenges to students, teachers, and school administrators. One of these challenges was how to manage the peak times of pedestrian movement, during drop-off and pick-up times, especially in dense urban campuses with inherent outdoor space limitations.

We utilized pedestrian simulation analysis to evaluate and develop strategies with school administrators. As the Fruin Level-of-Service (LOS) index is based on density it is quite relevant in understanding the density hot spots in circulation networks that will be problematic when implementing social distancing guidelines. In addition, Massmotion developed a "proximity modeling" tool, which allowed us to map areas that violate the social distancing guidelines. Proximity mapping is essentially a fine-tuning of the Fruin LOS to reflect a two-meter radius around each agent to reflect the social distancing guidelines. In addition, it is possible to track each agent in the simulation, and when and where they violated the social distancing guidelines. This level of information modeling helps test different drop-off schedules, use of different stair or entrance scenarios, implementing queuing areas where necessary.

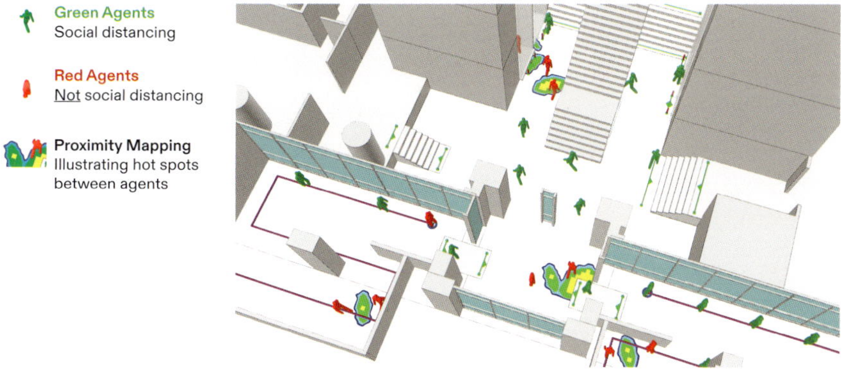

4.21 Simulation model by Efficiency Lab for Architecture. The agents coded in green that are in compliance with the social distancing requirements, and agents in red that are not. Proximity mapping is a calibration of the density mapping of Fruin Index to adjust for social distancing guidelines.

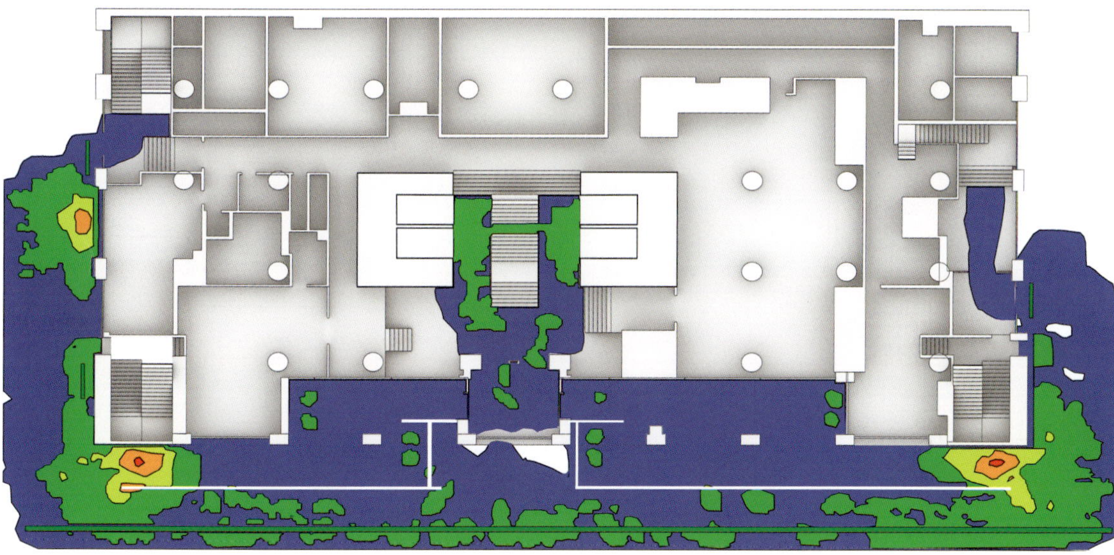

4.22 Pedestrian Simulation Study by Efficiency Lab for Architecture. Different density models tested, 400 students versus 600 students per 30 minutes. The density mapping shows the lower density eliminating bottle necks at the entry points and allowing for the social distancing guidelines to be implemented easier.

(B) Desire Paths:

A desire path is an emergent phenomenon found both in nature and human-made environments. It is the shortest and most convenient path within a given context, such as a goat trail winding along the contours of a hillside, animal markings in the snow, or the slowly emerging diagonal shortcuts across a campus green. (Figure 4.23)

This phenomenon is well recognized in the design and planning community. For instance, in university campus planning, planners might consider waiting on establishing predetermined student walkways, in favor of keeping them undifferentiated on day one, letting the paths emerge through the natural movement of the students over time, and then paving them once the paths are well established.

Desire paths are often applauded for the influence of the user in shaping the public spaces. It is inherently a bottom-up design approach, informed by the choices of the individual, as opposed to top-down decisions made by master planners. However, it is also a reactive process. The major elements of the physical environment, like the buildings, are already put in place, and the paths do not inform their shape and location; they are influenced by them. Desire paths are also criticized in fragile ecological environments, as they invite foot traffic wherever pedestrians choose to go. The ability to simulate the emergent phenomena of desire paths during the design process helps us to understand the relationship between the circulation and what is circulated, and it gives us the opportunity to inform the design. In other words, it allows us to shape the physical environment with movement.

Pedestrian simulation platforms using Social Force Model are based on desire paths. Therefore, it is feasible to simulate the emergent phenomenon of desire paths. And since we can simulate this, the question is how we can turn it into a design strategy that goes beyond paving paths that have emerged over time, toward shaping the physical environment in more significant ways. After all, the simulation allows us to run different spatial scenarios for emergent behavior and create feedback loops between the modifications in physical environment and the reaction of the agents to it.

4.23 (Left) Ridge trail. While not straight, it is the most convenient path as it avoids losing altitude in the topography. (Right) Diagonal paths between paved walkways are often observed as shortcuts between paved paths.

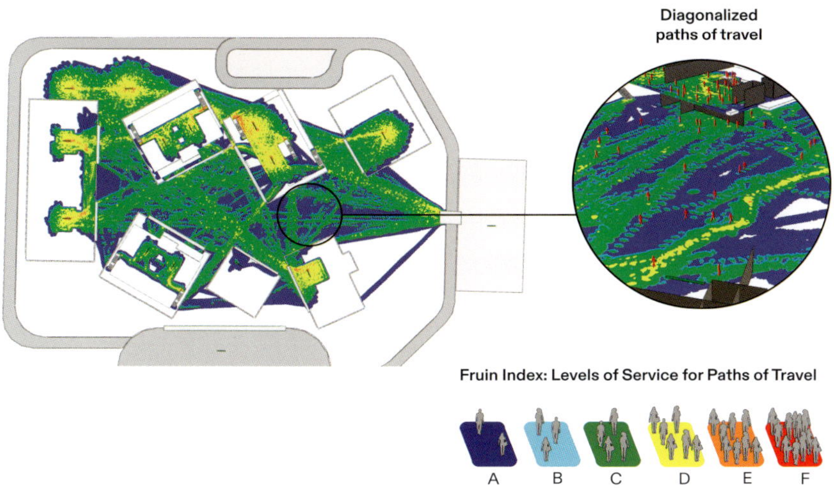

4.24 "Desire Paths" study for a Caribbean PK-8 School Campus by Efficiency Lab for Architecture. The building locations and functions were predetermined by an existing master plan. The analysis ran the impact of different interactions between buildings informed by programmatic relationships. The density mapping on the right shows the emergence of desire paths.

4.25 (Following spread) Overall view of the campus. The design is informed by the desire paths.

We tested the premise of designing with desire paths for campus planning. In the first case study, we ran a series of simulations on an existing campus master plan for a PK–8th grade school located in the US Virgin Islands. As part of the master plan, we were not allowed to alter the program or the location of individual buildings, but we could possibly shape the outdoor spaces, and refine the buildings to better integrate with how students circulate the campus. Given the intense precipitation of the tropical climate, the covered walkways would be a requirement, which made the understanding of how students move between the buildings even more important.

The initial study analyzed the student movement between buildings. (Figure **4.24**) We refined the subsequent model to include precise building entrance

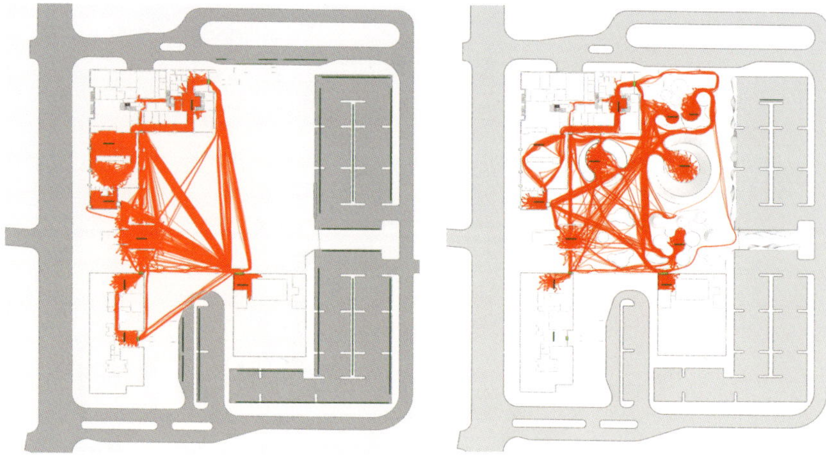

4.26 Campus simulation model by Efficiency Lab for Architecture. The image on the left shows pedestrian network without any landscape differentiation, whereas the one on the right shows the pedestrian network including attractors within the landscape. Careful addition of these "nodes" into the campus framework creates a more "labyrinthine" pattern of circulation that encourages discovery and exploration.

4.27 Aerial view of the campus showing the outdoor learning spaces.

locations tied to student schedules. Further iterations of the model showed an emergence of circulation patterns within the campus in diamond shape forms. These emergent circulation network patterns informed our development of the campus spatial planning. The covered outdoor walkways that created rain protected connections between buildings also enabled us to differentiate outdoor learning environments for different age groups. The differentiation of open spaces expanded to create protected areas, landscaped with native plants. The geometry of the building entrances and canopies were designed to respond to the circulation network, creating an architectural language informed by movement. (Figure **4.25**).

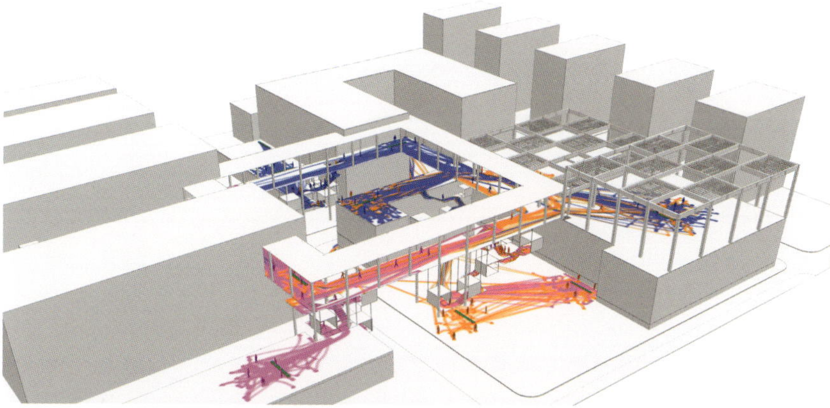

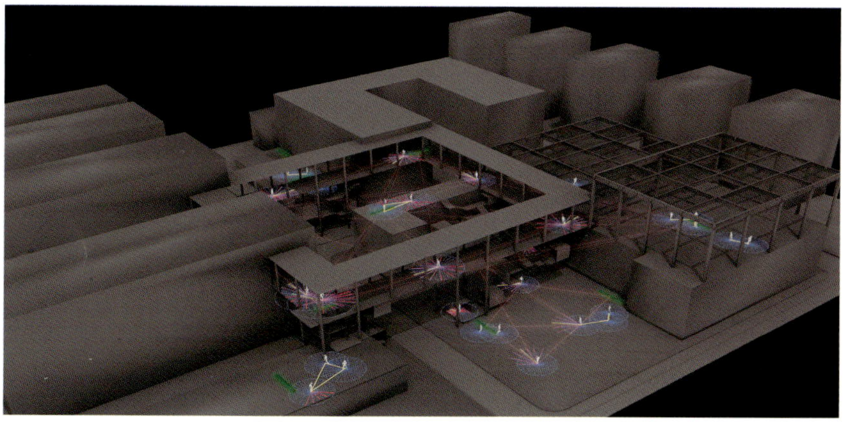

4.28 Pedestrian simulation analysis in between the buildings, roof playgrounds, bridges and the courtyard, by Efficiency Lab for Architecture.

For a nursery–12th grade school campus located in Miami, we expanded this idea of working with desire paths to include outdoor attractors, so that the agents in the simulation do not simply go from one destination to another but they encounter "places of interest" in between. The concept of creating these attractors helped to inform our design in conjunction with the programmatic requirements of the outdoor learning spaces. Some of the examples of outdoor formal and informal functional areas include outdoor classrooms, playgrounds tucked into the landscape, a bowl-shaped informal outdoor commons to encourage impromptu acting, landscaped niches for small gatherings, and learning gardens. The integration of these attractors into the movement space of the simulation transforms the emergent directional diagonal paths (Figure 4.26 left) into a more intricate web of connections (Figure 4.26 right). Through multiple iterations of the simulation, we explored the relationship between desire paths and attractors, which subsequently helped to inform the design evolution of the physical environment. In our final design for the campus, the landscape is shaped to encourage connectivity and exploration to enrich campus experience. (Figure 4.27)

For the design of a dense urban campus in Shenzhen, the relationship between desire paths and attractors were further tested to create a three-dimensional network of connections. Multiple buildings are connected through a network of elevated paths and bridges that weave together the interior and exterior spaces of the buildings. (Figure 4.28) Here, suspended learning pods within the bridge network, and outdoor playscapes on the roofs and in the courtyards of the buildings create a set of outdoor learning environments that acted as attractors in our simulation.

(C) Cafeteria Scene:

The high school cafeteria is arguably the place where the most complicated social interactions play out. In- and out-group bias, and bullying all take place within this physical space. Different grades arrive at the same communal space around the same time. The servery, where food is picked up by students, is typically a single-line formation and therefore provides high visual exposure—there is no place to hide.

At the end of the servery, at a single point of discharge, students need to make the most important decision: Where to sit? This moment has haunted many students and has become the subject of many stories in popular culture. For instance, in the movie *Mean Girls* (2004), Damian shows Cady, a new student at North Shore High School, a map of the cafeteria with labels for each table identifying the various groups. He explains:

> This map is gonna be your guide to North Shore. Where you sit in the cafeteria is crucial because you've got everybody there. You've got your freshman, ROTC guys, preps, JV jocks, Asian nerds,

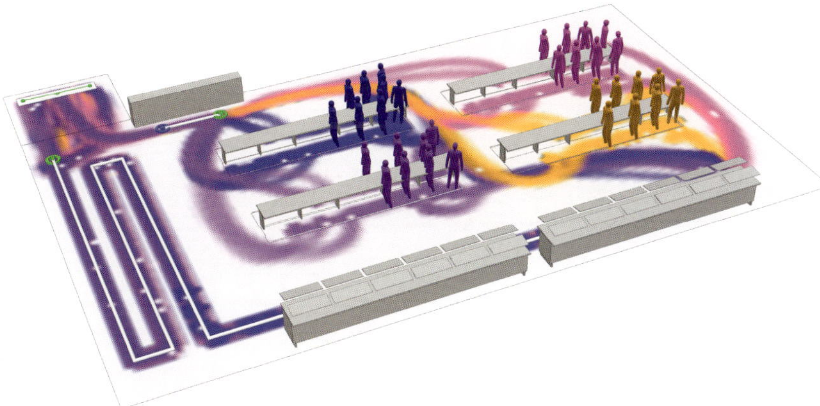

4.29 Cafeteria simulation by Efficiency Lab for Architecture. Agents in the simulation are biased toward their own groups. Each group is indicated with a color coding in the simulation. Regardless at what point agents enter the simulation, they avoid interaction with other groups and gravitate towards their own.

> cool Asians, varsity jocks, unfriendly black hotties, girls who eat their feelings, girls who don't eat anything, desperate wannabes, burnouts, sexually active band geeks, the greatest people you will ever meet and the worst. Beware of the Plastics.[33]

In other words, Cady's decision of where to sit (or where she'll be allowed to sit) determines which group she belongs to in the school. Dr. Julia Higdon highlights the problems of empathy when empathy turns into in-group favoritism and out-group derogation. (Refer to page 52) While cafeteria scene as it plays out in *Mean Girls* illustrates perhaps an exaggerated version, in- and out-group bias is a real concern in learning environments.

In the next case study, we modeled the cafeteria scene, acknowledging that the limitations of the simulation will not be able to capture the nuances of its real-life social complexity. We experimented by adding "repulsive" and "attractive" biases between agents in the simulation to get some insight on biased movement behavior. In other words, we attempted to simulate in- and out-group bias. Subsequently, we also tested whether we could break this bias in the simulation through modifications to the physical environment.

After the basic set up of the cafeteria queue in the model, we assigned groups in the simulation. As seen in Figure **4.29**, the different color-coded agents that represent different groups stuck together, no matter when they arrived at the cafeteria. An interesting characteristic of this finding was the influence of territory. Just as in real life, in- and out-group bias in the cafeteria implies a table for each group. Even though we were unable to shake off in-group favoritism and out-group derogation in the simulation, it is possible that one strategy to break this phenomenon is to break apart the territory, meaning that a changing seating arrangement may trigger reterritorialization. And the repetition of reterritorialization with no detectable pattern may result in breaking the group boundaries.

(D) Moving & Seeing:

When we move, our vantage points constantly shift and as a result, we continually see different perspectives. Although not exclusive, seeing is critical in developing spatial cognition.[34] As discussed in Chapter 3, the perceptual space (P-space) plays a significant role in human development. Understanding what and how we see as we move gives strategic input on how we can shape P-space. In the pursuit of designing for empathy, we can create P-spaces within which the choreography of movement is informed by what we see.

The Social Force Model applies vectoral forces to agents in a simulation, and an agent's movement is influenced by these forces. The simulation software allows us to map the gaze of the agents following the direction of their travel on vertical surfaces; this is called "Vision Time" mapping. The direct and peripheral vision of the agents are mapped in varying densities on vertical surfaces within their environment. In essence, the simulation allows agents to exist in the perspectival space. (Figure 4.31)

For movement planners and traffic engineers, the obvious use of this functionality is wayfinding. It allows them to determine the optimum location of signage, informed by vertical surfaces that are most seen by the agents in the simulation. Another potential use for this tool is to capitalize on the gaze of the pedestrians by using this data to strategically locate billboards, shop windows, or anchor stores.

For the purposes of this design research, Vision Time mapping provides important data points on spatial experience. The ability to map the vision

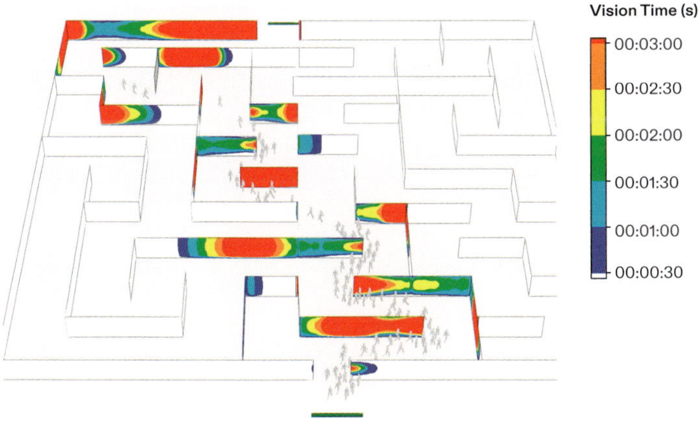

4.30 Labyrinth simulation model by Efficiency Lab for Architecture, showing the Vision Time Mapping in a meandering path.

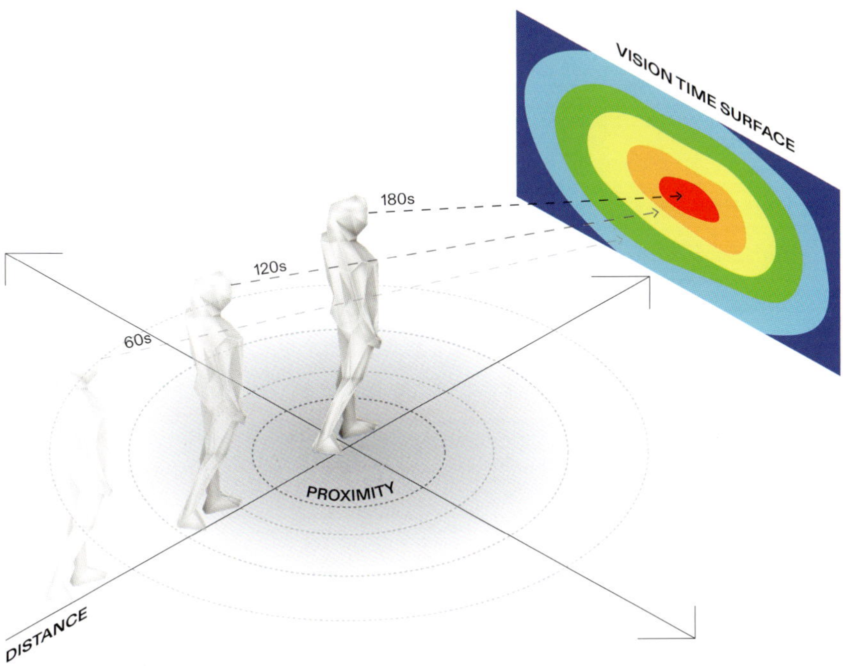

4.31 Like density mapping on floors, Massmotion maps the gaze of the agents as "Vision Time" on the vertical surfaces. The intensity of the mapping identifies the amount of time that the surface is seen by the agents in the simulation, changing from red (being the most) to blue (the least). White means no agents have looked at that vertical surface

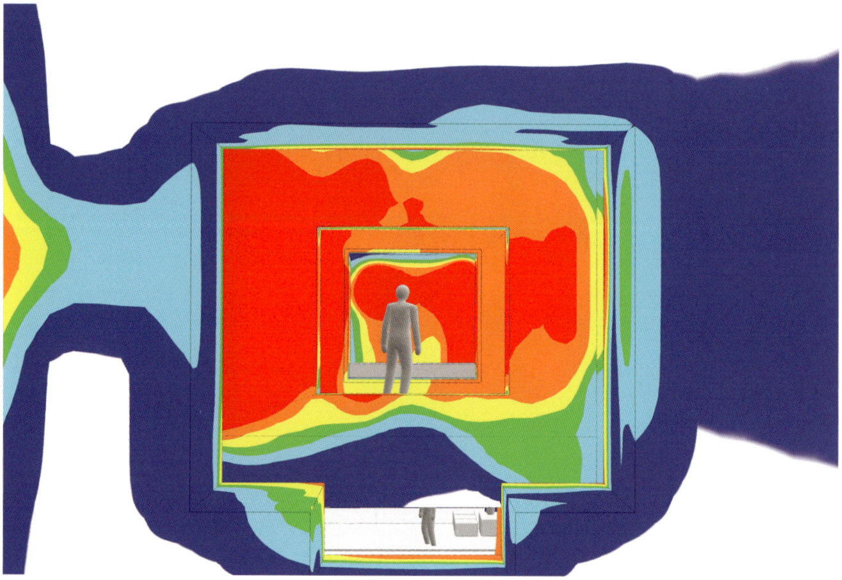

4.32 The “three niches” construct, as discussed in Chapter 3, is illustrated here with the Vision Time projected on the vertical surfaces.

of the agents effectively puts them in a simulated perspectival space. For instance, the analysis of the "three niches" construct illustrates the visual planes of interest as shown in Figure 4.32. In this single point perspectival construct, we can understand the relationship between movement and vision through space. The geometric construct of the deictic center as a four-dimensional space creates the reference for deictic expressions.[35] Vision Time mapping, which is based on the same geometric principles as the deictic center, creates a new set of data on the perspective of the agents. Where do they look as they move within the space? How long is their vision sustained?

Spatial experience is dynamic. As individuals move within a space, their deictic center moves with them, and hence their deictic expressions transform. [This] becomes [that], and in the continuum of moving deictic centers, the ability to shift perspectives from egocentric to allocentric frames of reference emerges. Being able to map vision through movement in space allows us not only to analyze how a space is seen, but also a way to design the space as shaped by the vision of its users. The premise of this approach is that molding spaces through carefully choreographed sights of vision will cultivate allocentric frames of reference that will, in turn, yield better places for social learning and hence catalyze empathy.

To study the relationship between movement and vision, we conducted a series of experiments. The first set of experiments considers vignettes that are not project-specific. They analyze the relationship of moving and seeing on paths, nodes, and stairs. The shape of the path informs what we see on that path. For instance, a straight path creates a singular visual focus throughout the trajectory of movement. Whereas in a path that bends, the vision of the person spreads across the concave surface while the convex surfaces receive no vision, effectively becoming a blind spot. Meandering paths allow the visual focus to shift in alternating directions. (Figure 4.34)

The second experiment is a comparative analysis of pinwheel arrangements versus cross intersections in circulation nodes. In a pinwheel arrangement, the vertical surfaces defining the node are highly visible by the approaching pedestrians in all four directions, whereas the cross intersections do not allow that. (Figure 4.35)

4.33 Vision mapping of an axial walkway. As expected, the agents gaze is straight to the virtual surface at the end of the axis. (Red shows the intensity of the vision time, and the peripheral vision is seen on the side walls.) Parisian Boulevards create these strong axial approaches marked by triumphal arches.

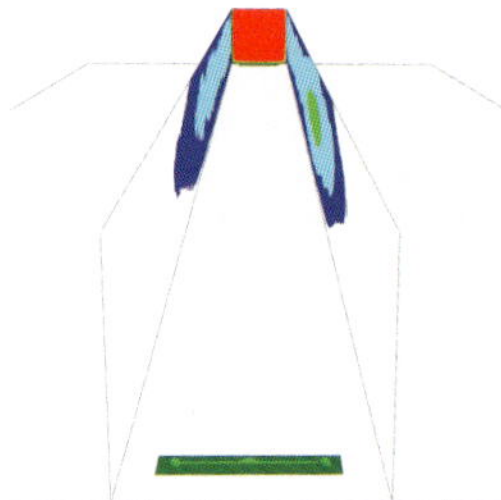

4.34 Comparative study of bending and meandering paths. As the path bends more, the axial focus vanishes and the vision surfaces spread across the concave surface. In contrast the convex surface receives very little to no vision, effectively becoming a blind spot. The meandering path removes axial view of the straight path, and instead alternates the visual focus from one side to another.

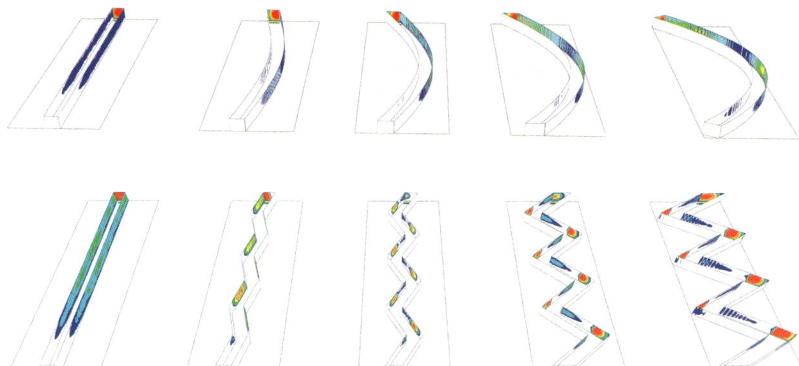

4.35 Comparative node analysis of a cross intersection versus pinwheel intersection. In the pinwheel node, the four vertical surfaces that face the approach become a visual focus, indicated by the red Vision Time. The cross intersection does not create a focal surface.

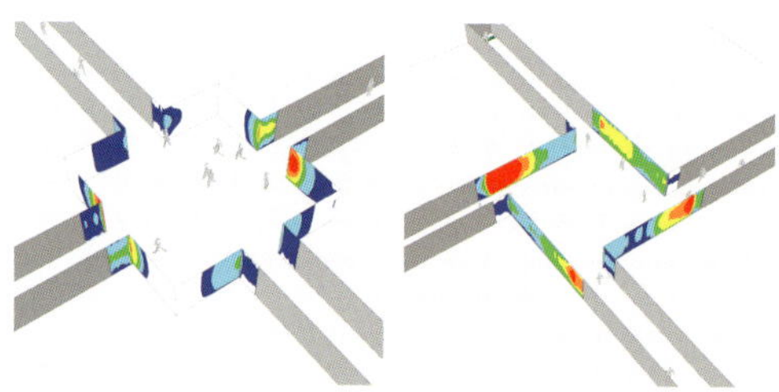

4.36 Staircase comparative study. The more bends between stair landings result in more visually activated surfaces.

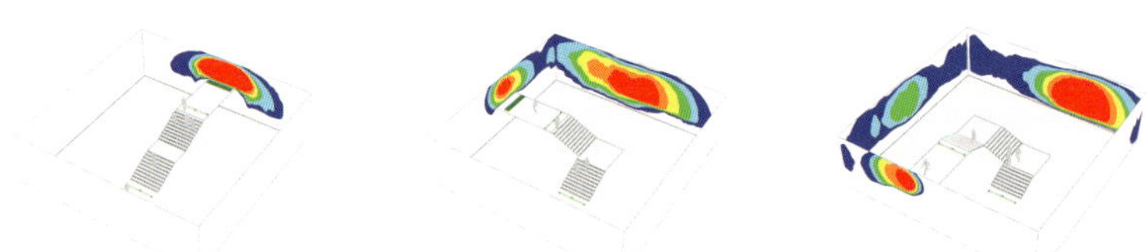

The third experiment analyzes what we see when we go up and down stairs. We tested different stair configurations—a straight run, L-turn, and switch-back. As seen in the meandering path, the more switches a stair provides, the more vision surfaces emerge on alternating walls, allowing multiple perspectives. (Figure **4.36**)

These three experimental vignettes illustrate the relationship between movement and vision mapping. Each one of these movement spaces creates its own unique P-space. For instance, the strong axial view on straight paths suggests a single point perspective. Not surprisingly, this type of axial arrangement in city planning is often used to show authority. For example, in the nineteenth century, Baron Hausmann, under the service of Napoleon III, led the reconstruction of Paris by cutting grand boulevards through the labyrinthine streets of the old city. The P-space of this new urban transformation reflected the authority of the Second Empire, and hence, one could argue that it has also shaped the L-space of Paris since then.

Is it possible to use Vision Mapping as a design tool? Can we sculpt space as if it was a malleable form that is shaped by the flow of people? In a series of experiments, we used Vision Time maps as a force of erosion that shapes the environment. For instance, we analyzed two streets as they divide a volume into three blocks. (Figure **4.37**) As pedestrians move around the blocks, their gaze is mapped on the vertical surfaces. The resulting Vision Time maps are utilized as a force to deform the blocks. The more intense the heat map—meaning more people are looking at those surfaces while they are moving—the stronger the force we applied to carve out the blocks. In other words, the building blocks are sculpted by the gaze of the pedestrians flowing around them.

This simple vignette illustrates an interesting conceptual shift: pedestrian movement is not simply flowing around rigid boundary conditions, but it becomes a force to alter those boundary conditions, like the flow of water shaping a slot canyon (Figure **4.38**). In this way, behavior is not only reactive, but it is interactive. This shift in thinking offers similar potential for pedestrian simulation to extend beyond a mere analysis tool that evaluates predetermined spatial conditions and provides feedback. Rather, it can have direct influence on the design of our physical environment.

4.37 Pedestrian simulation analysis by Efficiency Lab for Architecture. The Massmotion Vision Heat Map is connected to the Rhino Grasshopper script to erode the forms based on the intensity of the vision heat map.

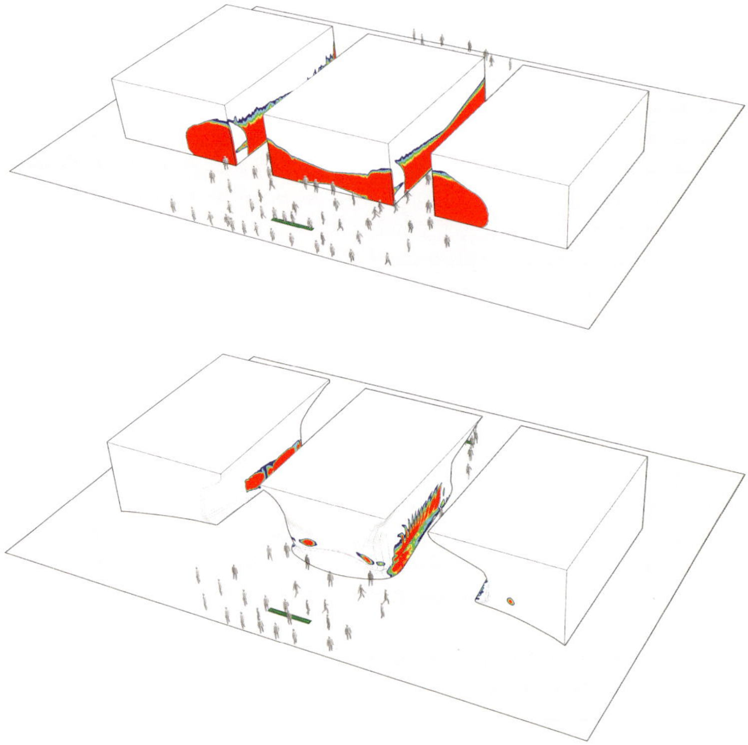

4.38 Antelope Canyon in Arizona is a slot canyon shaped by the movement of water.

This line of thinking led us to investigate how we can leverage the Vision Time mapping in the design of learning environments, where movement plays a key role in the daily routine of the students. The premise of this question was tested for an adaptive reuse project in Shenzhen, where we transformed an existing warehouse building into an Early Learning Center. The three-story warehouse was an efficient building for storing materials but was not as suitable for a learning environment. The deep pancake floors lacked connectivity. As we explored potential routes of connections between floors, we mapped the Vision Time of the students and teachers along these routes to create critical nodes of connectivity. Using Vision Time mapping as a strategy to erode areas in the floor slabs of the existing structure, we created a series of interconnected spaces. As these spaces physically blend into one another, they also visually connect across different floors through diagonal views (Figure 4.39), creating a sense of community for the school.

Through this transformation, new multi-level atria and interconnecting stairs weave together the interior of the building both visually and spatially. As seen in a strategic chuck model of the building's central circulation and commons space, Vision Time is mapped out on the vertical surfaces. The mapping clearly shows that the walls along the interconnecting stairs and the strategic slab cuts are receiving the most Vision Time as they bridge two or three floors. The existing warehouse structure "melts away" with the heat map of the intense gaze areas of the agents in the simulation, creating a highly connected spatial organization. A central cut-out space adjacent to the entrance of the building on the first floor forms a strategic location for a constellation of spherical light elements that bridge the two floors. (Figure 4.40) The central open area is the primary commons that allows for breakout spaces and more improvised pockets for learning and congregation. This space is also broken down with strategic niches to create more intimate environments that fosters a sense of belonging for the user. (Figure 4.44) These become experiential spaces for learning, both at the scale of individual study and for small group discussions.

The roof over the student commons was similarly eroded by movement, but this time it tracked the sun, to harvest daylight to penetrate deep into the space. (Figure 4.42) The central core of the building transforms from a dark and gloomy space into a welcoming, social learning hub flooded with daylight.

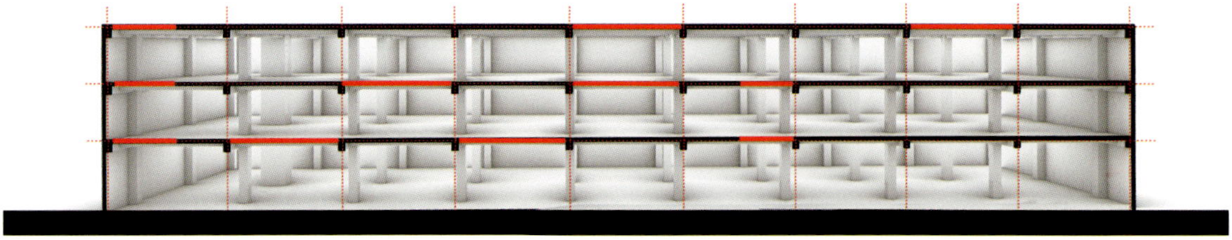

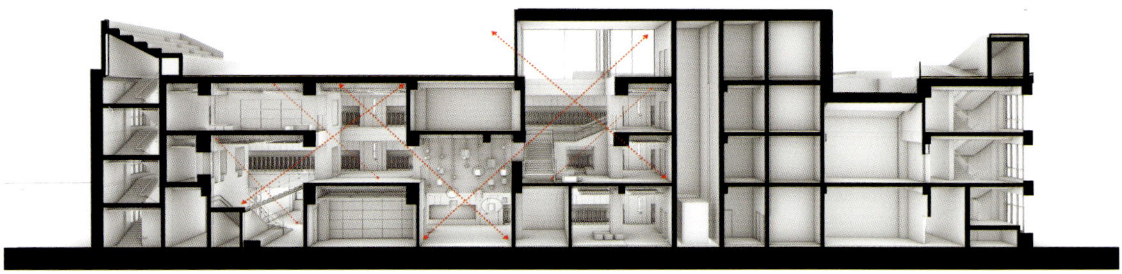

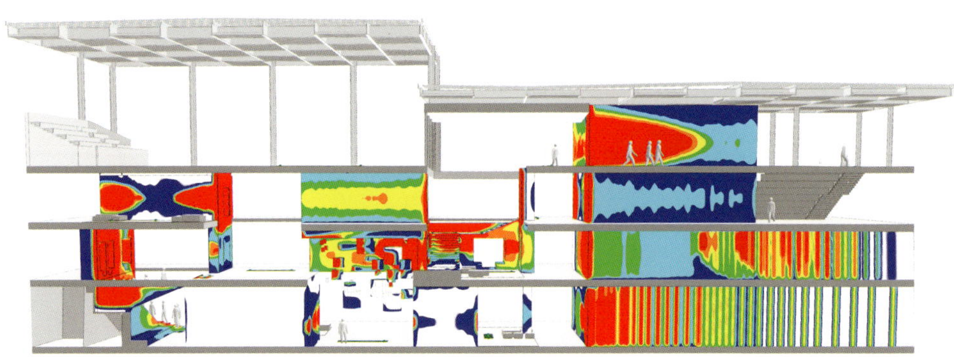

Avenues Shenzhen Early Learning Center introduces a design process to create learning environments that are informed by what people see as they move through space. Here, the perspectival space is shaped by the perspectives of the individuals within it. The potential of this design approach is the ability to curate interactions and create multiplicity of perspectives to catalyze social learning.

4.40 Student commons created by interconnecting atria.

4.39 (Facing page) The transformation of a warehouse into a learning environment by using Vision Time mapping.

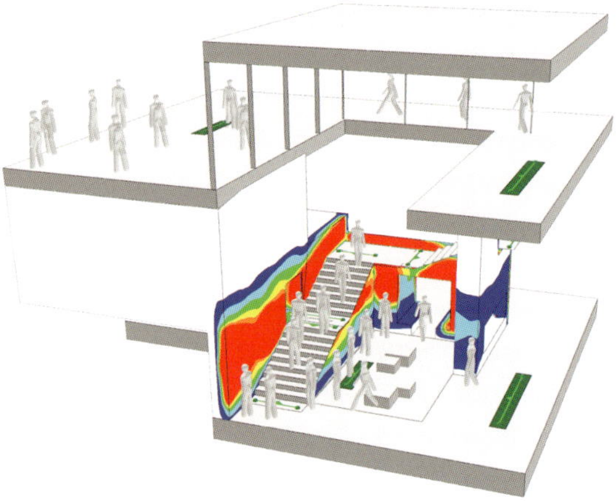

4.41 (Left) Daylight study; (right) Vision Time mapping on the atria walls.

4.42 (Above) Daylight studies to maximize daylight penetration deep into the Student Commons. Note the difference between the "before" image of the existing warehouse (left) and the "after" image (right) that shows the daylight penetration.

4.43 (Facing page) Daylit atrium and interconnecting stair at the transformed student commons.

4.44 Niches in the Avenues Shenzhen Early Learning Center allow children to have individual or small group activities.

SUMMARY: NICHES, FORUMS, AND LABYRINTHS

In the early stages of human development, movement plays a critical role in discovering our body, and discovering the world around us. The development of the sense of proprioception, the awareness of our bodies in space, begins in early childhood through the exploration of our limbs and understanding how to counterbalance them against gravity, as well as coordinate their movements. As toddlers develop their sensorimotor skills, they also discover the spaces around them by using their bodies. Various space exploration strategies, like insertion, help young children develop their understanding of the environment. This visceral relationship between the body and the environment is discussed in the Avenues Early Learning Center, toddler movement room case study.

4.45 Niches and forum: a student commons designed by Efficiency Lab for Architecture shows the integration of niches into the forum.

One noteworthy aspect of this study is the children's exploration of niches as places for insertion. The egg-shaped niches in the toddler movement room—characterized by an intimate scale, ergonomic geometry, comforting color, and soft materiality—are referred to as "bedrooms" by the children. This is particularly interesting when considered that the origin of the word "niche" etymologically comes from "nest" or "to make a nest." In evolutionary biology, niche construction theory discusses how species modify their environment to create their own habitat, such as creating nests.[36] The use of niches in this project creates a similar sense of place, a learning habitat for the toddlers.

The focus of this case study shifts from niches toward forums, as the discussion of movement evolves from explorations of the body to social interactions. In the Early Learning Center, the arrangement of niches around a central space creates a forum, a Zone of Proximal Development where children learn from each other.[37] The niches, defining the movement area in this project, establish a learning habitat that fosters the toddlers' development of sensorimotor skills by encouraging them to mirror each other's movements. As Albert Bandura pointed out, "In the social learning system, new patterns of behavior can be acquired through direct experience or by observing the behavior of others."[38]

In the context of social learning, we have explored the concept of niches and forums at different spatial scales, from student commons to campus quads. For instance, in Figure **4.45**, niches are suspended within the larger volume of the student commons, whereas in Figure **4.46** the niches define the edges of the campus quad. Both examples are organized around a forum to create a learning habitat that catalyzes social interaction.

The second half of this chapter focuses on navigation of spaces, and discusses how our perception changes as we move. The differentiation of movement—going from one point to another, and wandering around or drifting as a way of building new experiences—plays a pivotal role in the discussion. The Situationists' conception of psychogeography and drifting in the urban environment offers valuable parallels for learning environments. Explorations of our physical environment catalyze both individual discovery and social bonding, and they play an important role in the development of empathy.

As illustrated in the case studies, labyrinthine spatial networks with multiple attractor points shows the potential of how architecture of connections can foster empathy in learning environments. The lengthy discussions on pedestrian movement analyses illustrates the analytical processes in the design vignettes. It also highlights how the social force modeling used in these simulations share a similar geometric framework with the deictic center. In a way, these simulations put the deictic center in motion, and provide valuable analytical data, like mapping the gaze of the agents in the simulations on vertical surfaces. These types of analyses help to develop design strategies as

illustrated in the Avenues Shenzhen Early Learning Center where we shaped the physical environment with movement.

4.46 Forum as the heart of the campus defined by niches, designed by Efficiency Lab for Architecture.

Chapter 3 stressed the significance of how our P-space (perceptual space) impacts our L-space (language Space) and how, through careful perspectival constructs, we can nudge perspective taking as an empathy development strategy. This chapter builds on that idea and explores how our dynamic experience within the P-space through movement can be analyzed, and how it can inform the design of spatial environments for social learning.

MOVEMENT AND EMPATHY CHAPTER NOTES

1 Jean Piaget, *The Child's Conception of the World* (Routledge & Kegan Paul Ltd, 1971), 194–195.

2 Simon Gandevia, "Proprioception: The Sense Within," *The Scientist Magazine*, June 12, 2018, https://www.the-scientist.com/features/proprioception-the-sense-within-32940.

3 "Being-in-the-world" (*in-der-Welt-sein*) used in reference to Heidegger's phenomenological analysis of existence.

4 Indra Kagis McEwen, *Socrates' Ancestor: An Essay on Architectural Beginnings* (MIT Press, 1993).

5 Vitruvius, *The Ten Books on Architecture. Book III*, trans. Morris Hicky Morgan (Dover Publications, 1960), 73.

6 Vitruvius, *The Ten Books on Architecture*, 73.

7 Rudolf Wittkower, *Architectural Principles in the Age of Humanism* (Random House, 1962), 101.

8 Regardless of racial background and gender identity.

9 Rani Lueder and Valerie J. Berg Rice, *Ergonomics for Children: Designing Products and Places for Toddler to Teens* (CRC Press, 2019), 32.

10 Author interviews with the Avenues Small World teachers, New York City, April 2022.

11 Author interviews with the Avenues Small World teachers, New York City, April 2022.

12 The choice of naming may also have been influenced by how children climb up and down the netting, which has similar vertical movement as elevators. Elevators move, and for this age group, movement is associated with life. Calling the large egg niche an elevator gives it a sense of life and makes it a play companion.

13 David Elkind, *The Power of Play: Learning What Comes Naturally* (Da Capo Press, 2007), 108.

14 Carol Garhart Mooney, *Theories of Childhood: An Introduction to Dewey, Montessori, Erikson, Piaget, and Vygotsky* (Redleaf Press, 2013), 83.

15 Lev Semyonovich Vygotsky, *Mind in Society: The Development of Higher Psychological Processes* (Harvard University Press, 1978), 86.

16 Guy-Ernest Debord, "Théorie de la derive" in *Les Lèvres Nues*, 1956.

17 Simon Sadler, *The Situationist City* (MIT Press, 1999), 77.

18 Sadler, *The Situationist City*, 77.

19 Kurt Lewin, *Field Theory in Social Science: Selected Theoretical Papers* (Harper & Row, 1951)

20 John J. Fruin, *Designing for Pedestrians: A Level of Service Concept* (Polytechnic University of Brooklyn, 1970), 1.

21 Fruin, *Designing for Pedestrians*, 7.

22 Fruin, *Designing for Pedestrians*, 8.

23 "Zivile Sicherheitsforschung (IAS-7)," n.d., https://www.fz-juelich.de/ias/ias-7/EN/Research/research_node.html.

24 Bernhard Steffen and Armin Seyfried, *Modelling of Pedestrian Movement around 90° and 180° bends. Advanced research workshop on fire protection and life safety in buildings and transportation systems* (Santander, 2009).

25 Gregory Hoy, "A Comparative analysis of Agent-Based Pedestrian Modeling Approaches," Master of Applied Science Thesis, Department of Civil Engineering, University of Toronto, 2017, 6.

26 Dirk Helbing, "A Fluid-Dynamic Model for the Movement of Pedestrians," *Complex Systems*, 6, 1992.

27 Kurt Lewin, *Field Theory in Social Science* (Harper & Brothers, 1951).

28 Dirk Helbing and Péter Molnár, "Social force model for pedestrian dynamics," *The American Physical Society*, 51, No. 5 (May 1, 1995), 51.

29 Massmotion developed by Oasys—ARUP.

30 Massmotion, "The Verification and Validation of Massmotion for Evacuation Modeling," *ARUP* 1 (2015), 8–9.

31 Urban Space – AECOM, *Modeling Pedestrian Movement* (ICE Publishing, 2020), chapter 9.

32 Especially with the recent advance of artificial intelligence platforms and their presence in our daily lives, this is a critical question.

33 *Mean Girls*, directed by Mark Waters, written by Tina Fey (Paramount Pictures, 2004).

34 We engage all our senses in developing spatial cognition, and even though our sense of vision defines the perspectival space, our sense of proprioception—our awareness of our body—plays a significant role in locating our body and our movement in the perceptual space. People with visual disabilities develop different sensory spatial constructs that do not depend on the perspectival space.

35 Refer to Chapter 3, "Deixis and Empathy" in this book for the discussion on deictic center.

36 Kevin N. Laland, Blake Matthews, and Marcus W. Feldman. "An Introduction to Niche Construction Theory," E*volutionary Ecology* 30, no. 2 (February 3, 2016): 191–202. https://doi.org/10.1007/s10682-016-9821-z.

37 Vygotsky, *Mind in Society*, 86.

38 Albert Bandura, *Social Learning Theory* (Stanford University Press, 1971), 3.

5

PLAY AND EMPATHY

Toward an ecocentric perspective in early childhood

Play is immersed in all stages of our lives. We play with ideas, we play with things, we play with people. We can actively participate in the play, or we can watch other people play. It takes multiple forms; it can be spontaneous or structured. There are pickup games, sporting events, performing arts, role plays, imaginative plays, children's plays, etc. In our adult lives, play is often associated with pastime recreational activities that are not "work"; we either work or we "play." During early stages of our lives, on the other hand, it is not that binary. It is more visceral, and in fact, play is how we discover the world.

Friedrich Schiller defines play as a crucial human drive and he argues that it is only through play that we become human beings in the fullest sense of the word.[1] According to Schiller, play drive reconciles the two opposing drives we have as humans: the sensuous and the formal. The sensuous drive comes from our physical existence, or the sensuous nature of human beings. For instance, hearing a sound at a moment and anticipating the next sound to follow, is the nature of our sensuous drive. The experience is tied to the moment and bound to change. On the other hand, formal drive grows from our rational nature and strives for permanence. According to Schiller's philosophy, change versus permanence, sensational versus rational, feeling versus thinking, experience versus truth are the dualities between the sensuous and formal drives.

Play drive, on the other hand, reconciles the oscillations between these two opposing drives and establishes a point of equilibrium. The object of this equilibrium, according to Schiller, is "living form," a concept "serving to designate all the aesthetic qualities of phenomena," which he defines as "beauty."[2] Consequently, Schiller considers beauty to be the point of

5.1 (Facing page) Avenues São Paulo campus covered playground.

equilibrium we reach through play drive, and it is through beauty that we become true human beings.

Schiller's conception of play has a fundamental role in our lives. The perpetual conflicts between the sensuous and the formal drives are liberating for human beings, and through play we find that point of equilibrium between our feelings and our mind, so that we can experience concepts. This is perhaps best manifested in the arts, but it is not limited to it. Any explorations—whether physical, emotional, or cognitive, from experimenting with ideas to wandering around town—engage our play drive.

From a human development perspective, there is an authenticity to play. It caters to our curiosity, and the best forms of it can be observed in young children, where life is not yet tethered by any preconceived notions, but a pure landscape of discovery. As Vygotsy points out, for young children, play is a serious game, and when children play, the differentiation between imagination and reality does not exist.[3] Young children have not yet acquired enough data points to constitute what adults assume to be the real situations. Children discover the world through play, by using their imagination, like an explorer in a foreign land.

Combining Schiller's poetic philosophy of play, defined as a drive to find the beauty in life, with the emphasis of psychologists on play in early childhood as the most significant mode of learning, offers an opportunity in human development where the imagination of young children can shift an adult's grip on status quo perspectives.[4] For instance, through imaginative play, young children can develop personal connections with nature and build a genuine understanding that human beings are part of a larger ecosystem—a simple fact that adults seem to have a hard time internalizing. Through play, they can shift their perspective of looking at the world away from an anthropocentric view, and toward an ecocentric perspective.

The power of play is so visceral for young children that the development of empathy with nature through play can provide them with a profound perspective in life. This life-changing potential nudged this chapter toward focusing the discussion on play and empathy for young children. On the other hand, narrowing the discussion of play toward empathy with nature seems equally potent, because during early stages of development, a lack of categories in our thinking makes our world view unpresumptuous. For instance, young children have not yet acquired the binary oppositions of humans versus nature, and through play they can develop in-group empathy that sees nature and humans as part of the same team: the team of the living.

PLAY AND DEVELOPMENT

Play has a significant role in the physical, intellectual, emotional, and social development of human beings. David Elkind's development theory of play combines Jean Piaget's intellectual approach with Freud's motivational orientation, and articulates how different stages of our development are shaped by play.[5] According to Elkind, "play is our need to adapt the world to ourselves and create new learning experiences."[6] At no stage of our development is this more accurate than in early childhood when a child discovers the world through play. According to Piaget, the inner curiosities driving the intellectual explorations of the child are the key in the child's cognitive development.[7] For instance, an infant gains an understanding of object permanence—that objects continue to exist even if they are not within the child's sensory field—through playful explorations such as repeatedly throwing an object outside their sensory field and observing when an adult brings it back to them. In early childhood, self-initiated spontaneous play is the dominant mode of learning. And it should be, Elkind argues, as at this stage of development it is critical to encourage children's imaginations, and to avoid structured games like organized sports.[8]

Play continues to have a significant role, at later stages of development, through rule-based games and institutionalized play during which "young people realize their creative potential by engaging in the performing or creative arts."[9]

PLAY AND EMPATHY

In the summer of 1954, at the Robbers Cave State Park in Oklahoma, a group of Social Psychologists led by Muzafer Sherif conducted a study.[10] Twenty-two boys between the ages of eleven and twelve and with similar backgrounds were divided into two groups. Prior to the start of the study, the boys did not know each other, so there were no pre-existing social dynamics amongst them. In the first stage of the study, each group stayed within their own area of the park without any interaction with the other group. In this initial phase, neither of the groups were aware that there was another group of boys in the park. During this first week, the boys did scouting activities that required team work to achieve goals. Researchers observed the development of strong in-group dynamics.

Distinct roles and leadership dynamics emerged within the groups. It was observed that being part of the group encouraged the students to expand their skills, for instance, in one incident, a student hesitated to jump from a diving board, but he plunged in after the encouragement of his peers. This incident encouraged yet another boy to jump into the water to swim for the first time in his life.[11] At the second stage of the study, the two separate groups were brought into competitive circumstances against each other. They played games such as baseball, tug-of-war, and tent-pitching competitions. During this period, the researchers observed the emergence of intergroup conflicts, including use of derogatory language toward the outgroup. The hostile environment between the two groups escalated to higher levels including fist fights and camp raids. Meanwhile, the in-group solidarity increased. This seminal study shows how quickly a group identity develops and how quickly intergroup conflicts emerges, even though, in this case all the children came from similar backgrounds.[12]

The third stage of the study conducted activities to reconcile the goals toward easing tensions between the two groups. Simply eliminating the competitive games and bringing the groups in contact with each other socially did not work to ease the tensions. In fact, during these "contact" sessions, the intergroup conflicts continued, such as using derogatory language against each other. To dissipate the intergroup conflicts, Sherif and this team introduced common goals for the teams to work toward. For instance, the water supply of the

5.2 The Robbers Cave Experiment. Two teams playing tug-of-war.

camp broke down (or, more accurately, it was staged by the staff as part of the experiment), which required the collaborative effort of everyone to be fixed. In another setup, the staff staged an incident with the camp truck. Its engine suddenly broke down, and the truck needed to be pushed. After some debate, one of the students suggested pulling out the tug-of-war rope, and having a tug-of-war with the vehicle to help start the engine. Noteworthy to highlight about this incidence is that by playing tug-of-war with the truck the two groups effectively created a third adversary (humans against the machine), which created a new in-group formation. The introduction of a third adversary as a conflict dissipation strategy is something that Sherif's team avoided for the setup of the studies even though they noted its efficacy.[13] A second important aspect, which is of more interest to us in this context, is the introduction of play and its efficacy in releasing tensions within the group toward forming a type of solidarity in an effort to create something good for the camp.

One of the social dynamics the Robbers Cave Experiment showcased is that team play catalyzes in-group empathy. The benefits of this can be seen in the context of Social Learning Theory. A strong identification with a group excels the individual to do better than they would otherwise do by themselves, as in the case of the boy who was encouraged to plunge into the water from the diving board. The individual benefits learning from a more capable or skillful peer, as discussed in Vygotsky's Zone of Proximal Development theory.[14]

In the discourse of play, especially with organized sports where winning is defined and clearly associated as a prize of achievement, it further incentivizes the group spirit. The strong in-group identity allows individuals to learn from each other and work together as a team, leaving their egocentric perspectives behind, and develop one that is geared toward the group identity. This could be seen as a positive instrument in physical, emotional, and social development. However, as strong as the empathy toward our teammates may bind us together, this type of empathy also encourages us to see the other team as the opposing side, which can lead to "out-group derogation."[15] As competition becomes fiercer, so does the hostility and aggression toward the other.

The strong emotional contagion amongst the group creates an empathy in overdrive, giving a powerful sense of identity of belonging to a group with not much room for critical thinking. This type of empathy lacks true perspective taking.

On the other hand, imaginative play has a powerful agency in perspective taking. If we go back to Friedrich Schiller's definition of play, there is a critical point of view for the discussion of empathy. When discussing how play drive negotiates between the two opposing drives, Schiller gives the following example:

> When we embrace with passion someone who deserves our contempt, we are painfully aware of the compulsion of nature. When we feel hostile toward another who compels our esteem, we are painfully aware of the compulsion of reason. But once he has at the same time engaged our affection and won our esteem, then both the compulsion of feeling and the compulsion of reason disappear and we begin to love him, i.e., we begin to play with both our affection and our esteem.[16]

In this incidence, through the agency of play drive, the compulsions of feeling and reason dissipate, nudging us to take a new perspective, which allows us to develop empathy for the other. Play drive helps us to break through the egocentric perspective of our individual experiences toward understanding others.

PLAY AND ARCHITECTURE

In the context of structured play, the discussion on play and architecture, such as sports arenas, is a stale topic, because the design of the physical environment is strictly dictated by the rules of the game just like the game itself. For instance, the game of basketball is played with a set of rules, which not only governs the actions of the players but also the design of the playing field and the larger structure within which it is embedded. Beyond the benefits of social learning, and the pitfalls of intergroup conflict if the games were to be overly competitive, there are no strong design levers to pull that will encourage perspective taking.

Playground design, however, can be more playful in the sense that the playing is not structured by predetermined rules of any game and, therefore, creating spaces that encourage imaginative play is possible, and even desired. In the context of human development, a successful architecture of play creates an environment where games are invented, characters imagined, and new narratives emerge.

There is tremendous potential for creating environments that will foster empathy in imaginative play. For instance, young children can create new narratives and take allocentric frames of reference to build new perspectives as they play. Moreover, particularly for early learning, there is a unique opportunity to create empathy with nature through play. As Schiller described, play is a powerful human drive and it gives us the power to shift perspectives. This shift in perspective can move us away from a human-centric perspective toward a more ecocentric perspective.

It is the thesis of this chapter that through play we can create empathy with nature, in purposefully designed learning environments for young children. As discussed in the previous two chapters, the key design strategy is to build nudges in the physical environment to encourage perspective taking. The following design vignettes illustrate examples of spatial nudges toward building an ecocentric perspective, and propose how these strategies, then, can be used to design play spaces.

CHANGING THE FRAME OF REFERENCE: FROM ANTHROPOCENTRISM TO ECOCENTRISM

In Chapter 3, I introduced isocentric projections as a new frame of reference that catalyzes pluralism of narratives. Different from the egocentric and allocentric frames of reference, the shift of perspective to a non-human anchor (such as the Berlin Wall fragment, refer to page 104) allows us to create new perspectives. What if we change the anchor to a natural being such as a tree? Will the isocentric frame of reference, with a natural being as its anchor point, nudge us away from an anthropocentric worldview toward an ecocentric one?

For a Community Information Center in the City of Miami, we developed a concept that revolved around two existing live oak trees located at the center of the urban site, which was previously a parking lot. Over time, the two mature oak trees merged into a singular canopy with two trunks. The trees represent a kind of nature that is caught in the midst of our anthropocentric world. They are the ambassadors of a wider ecosystem that is threatened by human activity. So, any discussion on empathy with nature needs to include ways to build a language with these ambassadors.

Our design locates the oak trees as the anchor point of an isocentric frame of reference. The spatial projections from the trees shape the physical environment in such that, when viewed from within, a person's spatial perspective is hinged off the trees. The omnipresence of the trees within every person's perceptual space, in every space in the building, serves as a reminder that the protagonist of the story is not the users of the building, but the oak trees.

A narrative that is constructed through the deictic center of the oak trees creates a spatial experience where the light coming into the building will filter through the leaves, the wind brushing through the canopy of the tree will create the acoustic experience in the courtyard, the cooling shadows provided by the canopy offers comfort from the intense Florida sun, and the roots, branches, and leaves are at the vanishing point of everyone's perspective. Furthermore, this heightened level of presence of the trees as the center of a building that will be used by younger children and teenagers, may nudge them

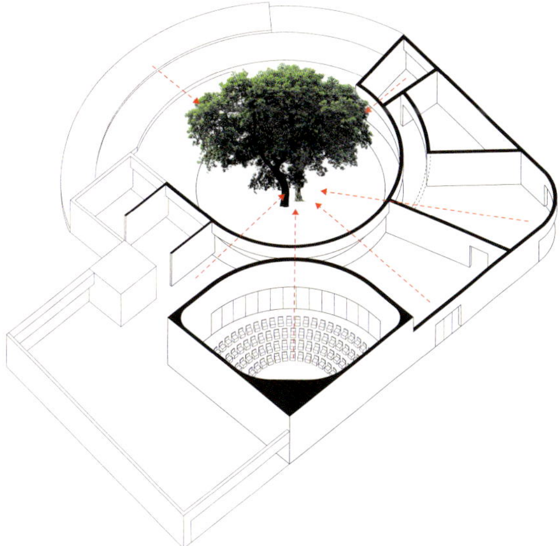

5.3 Avenues Miami Community Information Center. (Top left) Double oak trees on site; (top right) axonometric diagram of the building showing the isocentric projections; (bottom) physical model.

toward a deeper understanding of nature, which starts by communicating with these ambassadors of nature that are caught in the midst of our urban environments.

In the Avenues Shenzhen Primary School we established a similar dialogue with urban nature. In this adaptive reuse project, located in a dense urban context, we completely renovated and repurposed the existing building. (Figure 5.4) One of the central design strategies of the project was to create outdoor learning environments by activating the rooftops into playgrounds. The rooftops are transformed into a biophilic environment that utilizes natural materials and landscaping, covered with a series of light breathable tensile fabric roofs for a comfortable environment for the children. (Figure 5.6) The uplifting lightness of the roofs creates a memorable playspace for an age group that learns through movement.

The Tanglang Mountains surround the Avenues Shenzhen campus, and the larger of the three tensile canopies is carefully organized to frame the long vistas toward the mountains, while creating a shaded and comfortable outdoor learning environment for the students. The catenary curves of the canopy cable structure create a roof profile that counterpoints the silhouette of the mountains (Figure 5.7). There is an interplay between the lightness of the canopy and the permanence of the mountains. It is my argument that, this type of dialogue between the human-made and the natural environment within the urban context is an important part of the design lexicon that we need to develop, especially in spaces for self-initiated play, to encourage the children to develop a language of connections with nature.

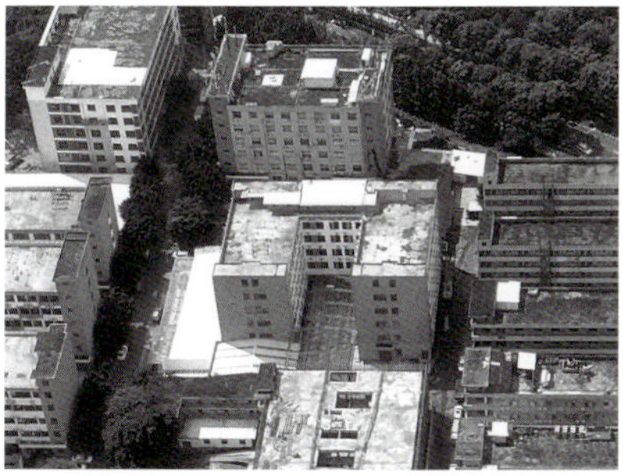

5.4 (Left) Before the adaptive reuse project; (below) after the adaptive reuse project. Note the tensile roof canopies covering the rooftop playgrounds.

5.5 Students exercising on the play structures not only develop their motor skills, but also develop social and spatial experiences. The tensile canopy that protects from the intense sunlight in Shenzhen, creates a dappled light underneath. The breathable structure of the canopy and the green wall along the side of the playground creates a biophilic environment. The integration of natural elements into the movement space is a key design decision for this age group, when children start to differentiate movement and life, which in turn creates an appreciation of nature and helps develop empathy with the natural environment.

5.6 Avenues Shenzhen Primary School. Note the Tanglang Mountains in the background.

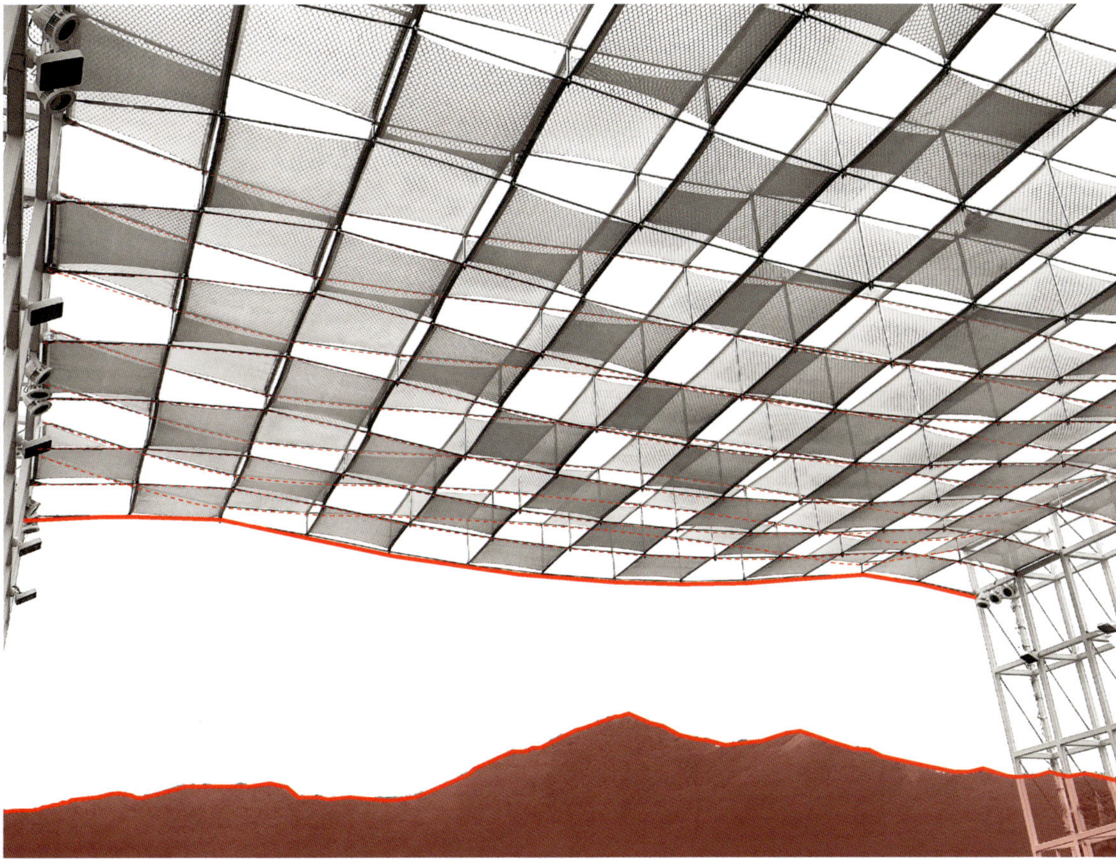

5.7 Avenues Shenzhen Primary School. Highlighted in red, note the counterpoint between the catenary curves of the tensile roof structure and the silhouette of the Tanglang Mountains.

5.8 (Following spread) Avenues Shenzhen Primary School roof canopy.

EMPATHY WITH NATURE IN EARLY LEARNING

What is nature? An adult's answer to this question could include examples of mountains, uninhabited landscapes, or scenes of wildlife to illustrate what is not made by humans, or everything in it that is not human. Cities versus countryside and buildings versus trees, for instance, can illustrate the binary thinking between the physical world that is made by and almost exclusively inhabited by humans, and everything else that is not.

However, for young children the meaning of nature is quite different. They do not draw clear distinctions between living and nonliving things. The concept of life is less categorical, and much more imaginative. In that imaginative world, they associate character traits with physical objects. For instance, as William Crain exemplifies a "loud truck may seem angry and a single cloud lonely."[17] Animism is characteristic of this age group. Inanimate objects are named, and they often develop a personality in the child's imagination.

Egocentrism is also a defining characteristic of early childhood. Young children think of everything from their point of view. Piaget explains that the child "believes all the world to think like himself. He has not yet discovered the multiplicity of possible perspectives."[18] There is a fascinating and imaginative discovery at play here. For instance, let us look at this classroom conversation referenced by Carol Mooney:[19]

> Teacher: I've brought in many beautiful things for our blue display. We have blue paint at the easel, and I've put 'Rhapsody in Blue' in the CD player since we are having Blue Day!
>
> Child 1: My mom's car is blue.
>
> Child 2: My mom's car is broke.
>
> Child 3: My TV is broke.
>
> Teacher (to Child 1): Your mom's car is blue?
>
> Child 1: I saw lions on TV.

5.9 (Facing page) Avenues Shenzhen Early Learning Center playground and the bridge integrated with the surrounding Banyan trees.

The improvisational quality of the conversation shows the complex associative flow from one topic to another in a paratactic way. The lack of syntax in the conversation is because the child has not acquired enough data points. David Elkind likens this state of early childhood to someone visiting a foreign country:

> because young children do not think in adult concepts and categories, they approach this new land from many different perspectives at the same time. They see this new world as an artist, naturalist, writer, scientist and much more. That's why young children are so fascinating to watch. One moment the child is a naturalist busily examining a grasshopper, the next an artist putting impressions on paper, the next a writer describing an experience in highly original language, and always the sociologist exploring the potential of social interaction.[20]

In summary, a young child's perspective on nature is far different from an adult's perspective. It is non-binary, in that it does not differentiate the human-made from the natural; non-categorical, as the systematic distinctions are not developed; paratactic, as it is not governed by overarching principles; personal, where cognition is highly situated from the child's egocentric point-of-view; and imaginative, where life can be attributed and found anywhere and can take myriad forms and shapes.

According to Elkind, children "learn primarily through play and direct sensory contact with the environment."[21] Environment plays a key role in early development. Therefore, shifting focus to the environmental context and its impact on the development of the children is critical for understanding how we can design learning environments that will foster empathy with nature.

But what is the environment? Gerald Lieberman and Linda Hoody argue, "the term 'environment' may mean different things at every school; it may be a river, a forest, a city park, or a garden carved out of an asphalt playground."[22] In their framework, there's an immediacy to the environment; it is a context that is tangible, relevant, and concrete to the experience. It is not limited to, nor differentiative of, natural environment but it is inclusive of the socio-cultural context within which learning takes place. And this framework, referred to as "Environment as the Integrating Context" (EIC) for learning, becomes a defining pedagogy, "that employs natural and socio-cultural environments as the context for learning."[23] Lieberman and Hoody clarify: "EIC-based learning is not primarily focused on learning about the environment nor is it limited to developing environmental awareness. It is about using a school's surroundings and community as a framework within which students can construct their own learning." David Sobel describes this as a "'pedagogy of place,' a theoretical framework that emphasizes the necessary interpenetration of school, community, and environment, whether it is urban, suburban, or rural."[24]

Like Lieberman and Hoody, Sobel also underlines that place-based education is different from environmental education.[25] The focus of environmental education is the broader environmental systems. The issues are too abstract for younger children to relate to and often, it turns into catastrophe education, in which, for example, a class on forests quickly becomes about deforestation. The children do not tend to build genuine relationships with the environment. Sobel argues that we need to give children a chance to love the earth before we ask them to save it. Like forest kindergartens, which originated in Denmark and became popular in Germany in the second half of the twentieth century, Sobel's case studies show young children spending extended times in the natural environment. For instance, in one case study, children at Sabot School in Virginia, go out to the woods regularly, to the same area, where they play self-initiated games.[26] The children are playing in two different areas of a dead log—at one end a group formed mostly by boys working on a deconstruction project of the log, trying to loosen the trunk from the stump; on the other end of the log, another group is building an imaginative chocolate factory and a museum created by leaves, branches, and saw dust. After some time, the group building the museum and chocolate factory approaches the deconstruction team; they object to their dislodging the trunk project, because they figure that if the trunk were to be dislodged that will destroy their chocolate factory and museum.

The conflict between the two groups resolves by the deconstruction group agreeing not to dislodge the trunk when there is somebody on it. This prompts one of the chocolate factory players to sit on the trunk to ensure that it will never be dislodged. In this fascinating example, self-initiated spontaneous play creates a learning experience integrated with nature, while prompting conversations on preservation (including learning to exercise nonviolent civil disobedience).

According to the advocates of place-based education, to build an emotional connection with the environment, this type of in-place and contextual participation is critical to ensure that the environment is not a generalized and abstract concept. For young children, abstractions do not help with their development. What is instrumental, however, is the ability to learn through specific experiences, as illustrated in the Sabot School example, and to be able to inspire new narratives from that context, such as the imagination of a chocolate factory on a tree log. Through imaginative play, children build relationships with the environment, which in turn helps them to relate and learn concepts of preservation. In this learning experience, the stories that are generated by the children are instrumental in building their relationships with nature. The stories form a crucial link between the specific experiences and the general principles.

Lave and Wenger articulate the significant role the stories play in the oscillations between generality and specificity. As such,

> Generality is often associated with abstract representations, with decontextualization. But abstract representations are meaningless unless they can be made specific to the situation at hand. Moreover, the formation of an abstract principle is itself a specific event in specific circumstances. Knowing a general rule by itself in no way assures that any generality it may carry is enabled in the specific circumstances in which it is relevant. In this sense, any "power of abstraction" is thoroughly situated, in the lives of persons and the culture that makes it possible. On the other hand, the world carries its own structure so that specificity always imply generality (and in this sense generality is not to be assimilated to abstractness): That is why stories can be so powerful in conveying ideas, often more so than an articulation of the idea itself.[27]

We can see the connection between Lave and Wenger's emphasis on stories in reconciling generality and specificity, and Schiller's concept of play drive that reconciles between the sensuous and the formal drives. The stories emerge when children build their own perspectives with the context, and how they learn about the environment. The stories are created through imaginative play.

To understand how to develop empathy with nature for young children, in the 2001–2002 academic year, at a kindergarten in Thessaloniki, Greece, a research study was conducted, testing 75 activities engaging nature with seventeen five-year-old preschoolers.[28] The theme of "forest" was explored in four modules: trees, animals, the risk to the forest, and the protection of the forest. The researchers used literature and role playing as empathy development techniques. For instance, children played games acting out the anthropomorphic characters in children's literature, where natural objects take human character. They compared their bodies to trees, finding similar characteristics between the roots of the tree and their feet; or the branches of the tree and their hands and fingers. They also watched puppet shows that further amplified role playing. Through interviews conducted before and after the study, the researchers found that the group that was exposed to natural environment and participated in emotional role playing showed a shift toward a more ecocentric perspective.

There are two interconnected threads on empathy and nature for early learning: one is the active participation of the young children in the "environmental" context, as defined by Lieberman and Hoody; and second is the power of stories and role-play as empathy development techniques.

The active participation in the environment plays a significant role in the development of empathy with nature. But what does this mean in terms of shaping the learning environments? Sobel's place-based learning framework is based on the necessity of interpenetration of school with its social and environmental context, and it suggests not only shifting where the curriculum takes place (i.e., regularly taking the children to forests) but also redefining what the physical learning environment should be like. From a designer's perspective, the interpenetration suggests a blurring of boundaries such as between the interior and exterior spaces, or between the school as an isolated institution and the school as part of a larger social-cultural context.[29] In this blurring lies an opportunity to engage the urban nature, which is referred to in the previous sections as ambassadors of the natural world, allowing a

5.10 Aerial rendering of the Avenues Shenzhen School showing the interpenetrations of the campus with its context.

deeper penetration of them not as a visual backdrop, but as an intrinsic part of the learning experience. One that defines the P-space (perceptual space) so potently that perspectives can shift from an anthropocentric toward an eco-centric frame of reference.

The second thread is the importance of stories and role play. How can designing learning environments catalyze imaginative play, so that emotional role playing and stories are generated through the self-initiated play? The juxtaposition of nature within a carefully curated P-space has the power, I argue, to foster empathy with nature that is both embedded and inspired from its very context; and thus offers a unique framework that allows young children to form their own perspectives and build their personal connections with nature.

VERTICAL PLAYGROUNDS AND PERSPECTIVE TAKING

The Avenues Shenzhen campus is located in Tanglang "urban village" in the Nanshan District of Shenzhen. In recent decades the local government's focus shifted from tearing down the existing historical contexts for new developments toward conserving the existing city fabric.[30] With this, a new design frontier opened in Shenzhen: the adaptive reuse of the Urban Villages, the complex dense developments with very intricate social, economic, and cultural structures that are woven into the urban fabric of the city.[31]

The urban villages of Shenzhen are the story of the empowerment of the rural community as opposed to the obsolescence of it in the face of urbanization. According to Juan Du, the urbanization of Shenzhen "was tremendously influenced by the transformation and the persistence of centuries old agrarian villages into the current 'urban villages.'"[32] Du attributes this power of transformation to the "large sociopolitical influence of the village collectives," a unique character of the villages of Shenzhen, different from the agrarian villages in other Chinese cities.[33] Shenzhen's urban village phenomena epitomizes the interpenetration of seemingly opposing elements into one another, in forming its complex and resilient organism that has evolved and sustained through constant negotiations. In that, the urban villages create a unique urban typology and an opportunity for a place-based learning environment that situates itself amid the ongoing perspective-taking between the agrarian and the urban, natural and the human, the old and the new. It is within this rich context of blurred boundaries and perpetual interpenetrations, that I will discuss the empathy with nature for early learning.

A first-time traveler to Shenzhen will be struck by how the natural environment—the dramatic topography and lush greenery—creates a strong counterpoint to the high-rise development that have sprung out of it. Most surprisingly, the unexpected presence of natural growth underneath highway overpasses or on concrete retaining walls shows the resilience of the sub-tropical landscape, overriding the human-made. One place to observe this interwoven relationship between the human-made and natural is in an urban village, like Tanglang.

5.11 Avenues Shenzhen campus site (highlighted in red) within the Tanglang Urban Village.

The Early Learning Center (ELC) is part of the larger master plan of the Avenues Shenzhen Campus designed by Efficiency Lab for Architecture, which interweaves seven existing buildings of the Tanglang Urban Village with porous groundscapes, elevated pedestrian bridges, and rooftop playgrounds. (Figure 5.12) Designing an urban campus that creates safe pedestrian connections while respecting the existing urban fabric is an important consideration of the project. And as part of this effort, the project creates a complex organism that negotiates the relationship with the urban fabric, blurring the ground plane from the street level to multiple levels of connections within and in-between the buildings and its context.

Within the densely settled urban village, the Early Learning Center courtyard was one of the few ground-level open spaces available for campus development, and as part of the master plan this space was transformed into the playground. This transformation brings into question an important problem: how can we interconnect the ground level open space with spaces at different levels of the campus? This pragmatic question brings us to a larger discussion of how buildings meet the ground, and the negotiations between the vertical axis of the buildings and the horizontal axis of the urban context.

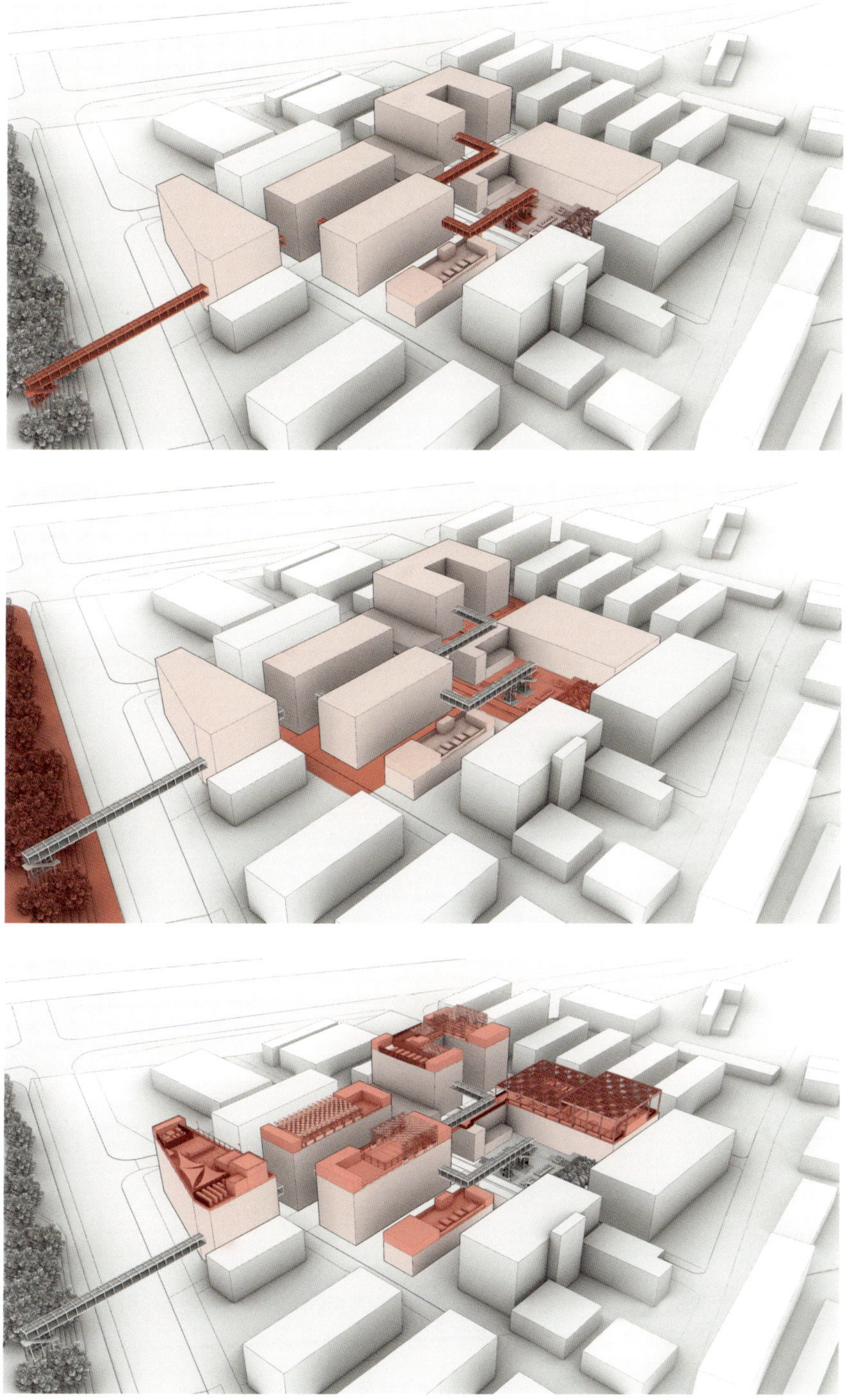

5.12 (Top) Bridges connect the campus buildings to create an elevated and safe campus walk. The network of bridges also connects the campus to the nearby adjacent park; (center) ground spaces are activated to create playgrounds and private/public open spaces that engages the context; (bottom) the roof terraces are activated to create playgrounds and outdoor learning environments. The lightweight canopies are designed to provide shade for a more comfortable environment. The learning spaces are designed to connect with the context and situate the campus in its specific environment.

5.13 (Left) Aerial photo showing the site of the Early Learning Center and the courtyard within the dense urban fabric of Tanglang. (Right) The parking lot before it was transformed into the Early Learning Center playground.

French urbanist and architect Paul Virilio critiqued that the vertical and horizontal organizations separated buildings from their urban context.[34] According to Virilio, the village as a settlement was characterized by its horizontality whereas the evolution of the modern cities, like New York, prioritized the verticality at the expense of the horizontal plane and thus disconnecting the building from its context. Virilio brings into this dichotomy a new axis, the oblique, to negotiate these two conditions.

He writes,

> And we are now confronted by the overriding necessity to accept as a historical fact the end of the vertical as axis of elevation, the end of horizontal as permanent plan, in order to defer to the oblique axis and the inclined plan, which realize all the necessary conditions for the creation of a new urban order and permit as well a total reinvention of the architectural vocabulary. This tipping of the plane must be understood for what it is: the third spatial possibility of architecture.[35]

The oblique axis in its most literal interpretation manifests in ramps or sloped planes that negotiated different levels of buildings and their connections to the urban context. However, Virilio's "third spatial possibility of architecture" is conceptually more potent as a "space of negotiations" than a sloping plane. The dichotomy between the horizontal and vertical, or the agrarian and the

5.14 The parking lot after it was transformed into the Early Learning Center playground.

urban—as pointed out by Virilio to be the primary axis of each settlement typology—is noteworthy for our discussion, in that the agrarian villages of Shenzhen evolved through the negotiations between these two forces into becoming urban villages. Therefore, in integrating the different levels of the school into the fabric of the urban village, the notion of the Oblique Function as a space of negotiations plays an important conceptual role for the design of the project.

Returning to the question of how the ELC playground can connect to the different levels of the campus, we looked at the the approach of blurring the ground—not in the form of a grand sloping plane but into something more intricate, such as how a banyan tree blurs its roots and branches. The reference to the banyan tree is intentional in both a literal and metaphorical sense. The ELC playground is lined by a row of banyan trees. Their intricate root and branch structure define the edge of the campus. The engagement with this intricate organism allows for blending the boundaries of the playground and creates opportunities for children to engage with the trees.

5.15 (Left) Banyan tree in Lahaina, Maui. As this book was getting ready for publication, the historic Banyan tree in Maui was severely burnt in the tragic fire, but reportedly still shows signs of life. (Right) Trunk structure of the Banyan tree on the Avenues Shenzhen campus.

As a design strategy, the blending of the school playground with the banyan trees play a significant role in situating the school in its unique environment.[36]

On the other hand, the metaphor of the banyan tree blurring the lines between the vertical and horizontal axis is quite rich, because a banyan tree is not a normal tree. It is an extraordinary organism, which starts its life as an epiphyte on a branch of a host tree, and through a complex relationship with its environment (for example, feeding from the moisture and minerals off the bark of the host tree), it grows downwards to form its own roots. It follows multiple growth trajectories, creating a lattice. The multiplicity of the interconnected trunks and branches create a field condition as seen in the Lahaina banyan tree, where it becomes hard to differentiate where one tree ends and the other one begins. (Figure 5.15) Walking underneath the banyan canopy, one feels the sense of the upside-down growth pattern. The differentiation between the trunk and the branch is blurred.

The interconnecting bridges between the buildings of the Avenues Shenzhen campus utilize a design strategy analogous to the intricate upside-down spatial growth of the banyan trees. This is achieved through structural configurations arranged in rigorous geometric arrangements. A three-dimensional grid matrix is established to organize the Vierendeel truss

5.16 "Klein 'Labyr,'" model of Constant's New Babylon. Constant imagined a world without borders and constraints. It was the "play drive" that liberated the people. The physical manifestation of this idea is represented in models that showed spatial fluidity and perpetual interpenetrations where there are no set boundaries.

structure of the bridge.[37] The subdivision of the grid members into smaller squares establishes a recursive character of the fractal geometry that creates the intricate organization of the structural elements. The logic of the Vierendeel truss merging into the columns blurs the lines between the support and that which is supported, giving a continuum to the bridge experience as it passes through the banyan trees. The spiraling stairs that wrap around the vertical members create a spatial continuity of circulation between levels. And the diagonal steel members of the stair form a geometric counterpoint to the three-dimensional Cartesian grid. As the bridge negotiates different horizontal levels of the campus, the columns and the beams merge into one another, forming a complex and ambiguous organism. The elements of the bridge suggest a sense of upside-down growth like the banyan tree, as the spaces within the bridge appear to be suspended. This labyrinthine spatial structure is occupiable at multiple levels, which in effect creates a "space

5.17 (Left) Axonometric view of the bridge that weaves in between the banyan trees and connects multiple buildings. (Right) Close-up axonometric view of the Vierendeel truss and the supporting structure of the bridge.

of negotiations" between the horizontal and the vertical axes, or between the context and the school. The key functional element of this space of negotiations is a new typology: the vertical playground.

The vertical playgrounds create an environment for discovery that juxtaposes the playscapes with the banyan trees, allowing children to see this fascinating organism through different spatial frames of reference. "Play" is the critical activator of this spatial construct because it is only through play that we can blur the lines between nature and architecture both physically and imaginatively. As children climb up and down the ladders or move down the slides, they see different parts of the tree in their perspectival space. When they walk at the bridge level, they pass through the canopy of the tree, observing the strangling branches growing downwards toward the ground. The architecture of the vertical playgrounds does not try to mimic nature formally. In fact, the choice of materiality and color is designed to differentiate the structure from the trees. However, the structure becomes an armature to encourage the children to experience the nature. Its purposefully choreographed elements are designed to integrate the banyan tree into the P-space, so that the children's self-initiated play in these intricate, labyrinthine spaces can construct an L-space that builds connections with nature.

As discussed earlier, there are two conceptual threads to empathy and nature for young children. One is the engagement with the environment and the second one is the use of the stories and role playing as a technique of empathy development. The deliberate design strategies of the vertical playgrounds create a spatial environment of engagement with the banyan trees through proximity,

5.18 Construction of the Avenues Shenzhen bridge Vierendeel truss.

framing, and juxtapositions. (refer to Figure 5.21) It blurs the boundaries between the human-made and natural, and it creates interpenetrations with the context as favored by the advocates of place-based education. On the other hand, the spatial echo between the intricate members of the bridge structure and the interlaced branches and trunks of the surrounding banyan trees, is deliberately created to nudge the children for perspective taking.[38] As observed in the self-initiated games of the children, the vertical playgrounds are often named "the base," safe hiding place, suggesting a story around a tree and a treehouse.[39] It is my theory that this type of spatial engagement with urban nature through self-initiated play has a rich potential to create stories, which is key to developing empathy with nature.

5.19 The bridge coming through the banyan trees that line up the edge of the Early Learning Center playground. The structural configuration of the stair and the colored boxes create the sense of suspension, which blurs the line between the supported and the support.

5.20 The bridge structure crossing the road allowing for safe connections between the buildings while allowing children views of the banyan canopy.

1

2

3

6

7

8

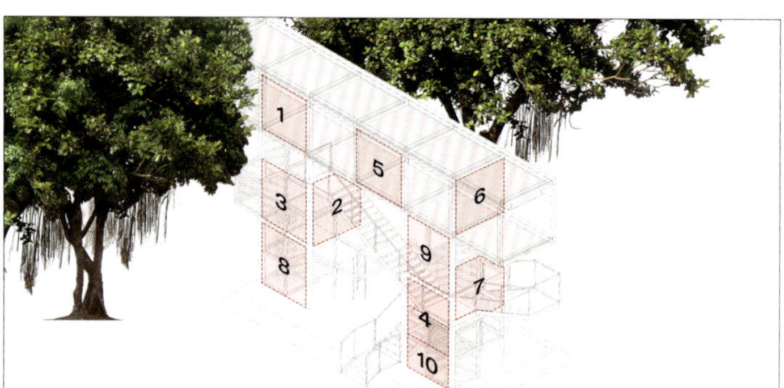

4

5

9

10

5.21 Proximity, framing, and juxtapositions: different frames of experience within the vertical playgrounds allow for multiple perspectives toward the banyan trees.

The key image shows the location of different perspectives. The three-dimensional matrix of frames allows for multiple reference points toward the banyan tree. Even though the bridge does not form a radial "isocentric spatial frame of reference," the multiplicity of views from different levels acts similarly in constructing a varied experience with the banyan trees, nudging the children toward a more ecocentric point of view.

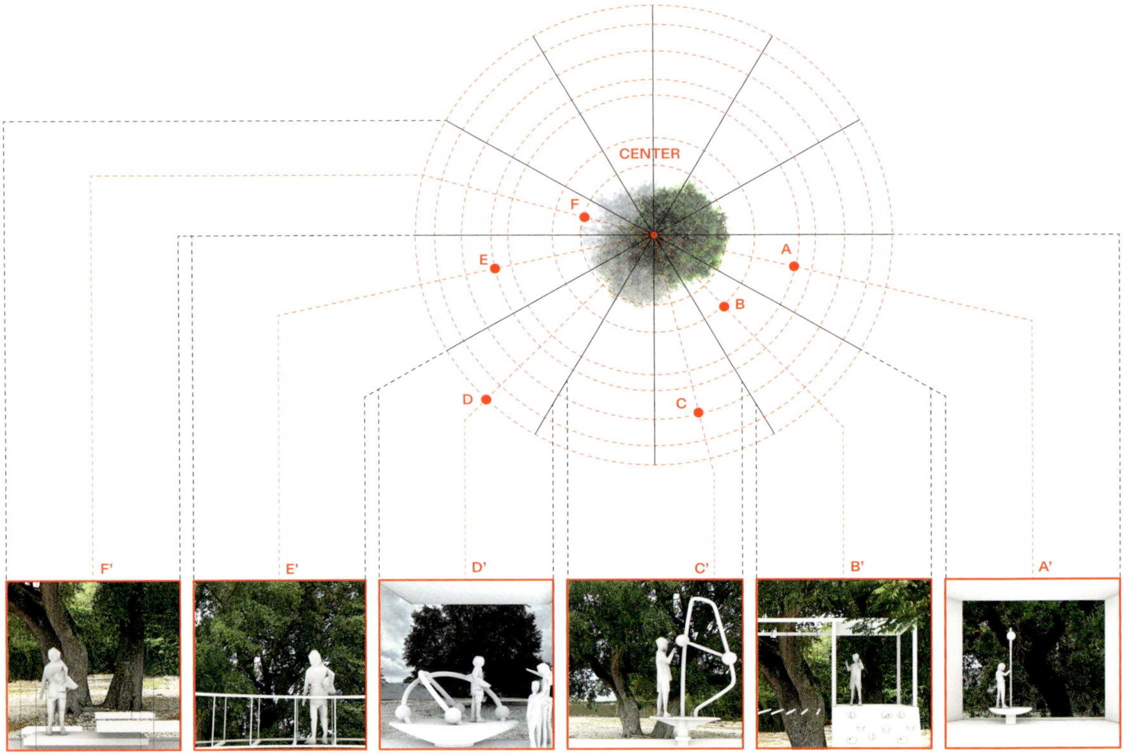

5.22 Unfolding the isocentric spatial frame of reference onto separate perspectival frames. Double oak trees that anchor the center of the projections in the Miami Community Information Center project are experienced through multiple perspectives. The strategy of unfolding the isocentric projections onto a grid, formed the conceptual basis of Avenues Shenzhen vertical playgrounds.

SUMMARY: NARRATIVES THROUGH PLAY

In the larger discussion of development of empathy through play, there are two reasons to focus on empathy and nature for young children. The first one is the difficulty of building empathy with nature in later stages of development. Due to centuries of cognitive bias, shifting from an anthropocentric to an eco-centric perspective requires a heavy cognitive burden for adults. Modernity has cemented the dichotomy of human versus nature in all aspects of our lives, and it has created a world where in-group and out-group derogation is embedded in our relationship with nature. Both the embrace and the critique of this position is present in philosophy and literature. For instance, the infamous Nietzsche anecdote in Turin, through storytelling finds its way into Milan Kundera's novel *Unbearable Lightness of Being*.[40] It is the philosopher's critique against Descartes's rationalism. Kundera writes:

> Seeing a horse and a coachman beating it with a whip, Nietzsche went up to the horse and, before the coachman's very eyes, put his arms around the horse's neck and burst into tears.
>
> That took place in 1889, when Nietzsche, too, had removed himself from the world of people. In other words, it was at the time when his mental illness had just erupted. But for that very reason I feel his gesture has broad implications: Nietzsche was trying to apologize to the horse for Descartes. His lunacy (that is, his final break with mankind) began at the very moment he burst into tears over the horse.[41]

Nietzsche's mental breakpoint is also the breakpoint of anthropocentrism. This allegorical story, in one way of reading, illustrates the cognitive burden that it requires to break away from the egocentric perspective of humankind. This is also where our play drive in early childhood presents itself as an opportunity to bypass this cognitive bias before it establishes itself in the later stages of development.

In the discussion of play and empathy, the second reason why we should focus on empathy and nature in young children is because of the significance of play in early childhood. The non-structured imaginative play is the purest manifestation of our play drive. Later in life, our play drive operates in the background, sometimes subdued, and often institutionalized through organized activities. However, young children do not categorize nature the way adults do, and in their imaginative play, nature blends in as an extension of life.

This chapter references back to the isocentric spatial frame of reference, introduced in Chapter 3 (refer to page 102), as a spatial strategy to develop empathy with nature. The isocentric spatial frame of reference establishes a deictic center for a non-human anchor, from which multiple perspectives could be created. In other words, it takes the power of our egocentric construct—our default mode—and multiplies it to create a pluralistic point of view. This type of projection was illustrated in the Miami Community Information Center. By locating the double oak trees at the anchor point, the trees become the protagonist of the narrative for the project, and by that, they nudge people toward the development of in-group identity with nature.

On the other hand, the vertical playgrounds in Avenues Shenzhen Early Learning Center unfold the multiplicity of perspectives of the isocentric frame of reference, into a three-dimensional grid that wraps around the Banyan Trees. (Figure 5.22) This type of unfolding is common in projective geometry, and as Robin Evans stated, the projections are instrumental in connecting thinking and imagination.[42] The children playing within the intricate grid of the play structure, in each one of these frames, experience different perspectives of the Banyan trees at different scales that is juxtaposed onto their own perspectival space. The boundaries between the tree and the play structure are blurred, for new narratives to emerge. This intricate play structure creates interpenetrations between the horizontal and vertical plane (as advocated by Virilio[43]), as well as the school and its context (as advocated by place-based education[44]).

PLAY AND EMPATHY CHAPTER NOTES

1 Friedrich Schiller, *Essays: Letters on the Aesthetic Education of Man* (The Continuum Publishing, 1993).

2 Schiller, *Essays*, 128.

3 Lev Semyonovich Vygotsky, *Mind in Society: The Development of Higher Psychological Processes* (Harvard University Press, 1978), 104.

4 David Elkind, *The Power of Play: Learning What Comes Naturally* (Da Capo Press, 2007).

5 Elkind, *The Power of Play*, xii.

6 Elkind, *The Power of Play*, 3.

7 Carol Garhart Mooney, T*heories of Childhood: An Introduction to Dewey, Montessori, Erikson, Piaget, and Vygotsky* (Redleaf Press, 2013), 80.

8 Elkind, *The Power of Play*, 81.

9 Elkind, *The Power of Play*, 10.

10 Muzafer Sherif, et al., *The Robbers Cave Experiment: Intergroup Conflict and Cooperation* (Wesleyan University Press, 1954).

11 David Berreby, *Us & Them: The Science of Identity* (The University of Chicago Press, 2005), 171.

12 The influence of diverse backgrounds for intergroup conflicts was studied by other scholars. "In 1963, Lutfy N. Diab tried to repeat the Robbers Cave procedure with eleven-year-old boys in Beirut. Eight were Christians, and ten Muslims. Not surprisingly, given the historic tensions between religious communities in Lebanon, fighting broke out between the two teams of campers, the Blue Ghosts and the Red Genies....The striking fact about this camp, though, is that the fighting was not along religious lines. The Blue Ghosts consisted of five Muslims and four Christians; so did the Red Genies...Fourteen of the eighteen campers had come from fiercely religious schools, yet in the camp, separated from the outside world, when they could easily have chosen to see themselves as Christian versus Muslim, they chose instead Ghost versus Genie." Berreby, *Us & Them*, 178.

13 Sherif, et al., *The Robbers Cave Experiment*, 151.

14 Vygotsky, *Mind in Society*, 86.

15 See Dr. Julia Higdon, "Empathy in Perspective," in this book on pages 41–60.

16 Schiller, *Essays*, 127.

17 William Crain, *Theories of Development* (Routledge, 2016), 135.

18 Jean Piaget, *The Child's Conception of the World* (Routledge & Kegan Paul Ltd, 1971), 167.

19 Mooney, *Theories of Childhood*, 86.

20 Elkind, *The Power of Play*, 116–117

21 Crain, *Theories of Development*, 144.

22 Gerald A Lieberman and Linda L. Hoody, *Closing the Achievement Gap: Using the Environment as an Integrated Context for Learning* (State Environment and Education Roundtable, 1998), 7.

23 Lieberman and Hoody, *Closing the Achievement Gap*, 7.

24 David Sobel, *Place-Based Education* (The Orion Society, 2004), 17.

25 Sobel, *Place-Based Education*, 13.

26 David Sobel, presentation at Thatcher Montessori School, https://www.davidsobelauthor.com/speaking (00:48)

27 Jean Lave and Étienne Wenger, *Situated Learning: Legitimate Peripheral Participation* (Cambridge University Press, 1991), 33–34.

28 Loukia Lithoxoidou, et al., "Trees Have a Soul Too!: Developing Empathy and Environmental Values in Early Childhood," *International Journal of Early Childhood Education*, 2017.

29 Lave and Wenger, *Situated Learning*, 39–40.

30 Juan Du's book, *The Shenzhen Experiment: The Story of China's Instant City*, published in 2020, lays a critical framework for the analysis of urban villages of Shenzhen and the significant role they played in the city's history.

31 "In November 2016, Shenzhen released a new urban planning policy, 'The 13th Five-Year Plan of Shenzhen Urban Renewal,' which indicated that the government no longer viewed demolition and redevelopment as the predominant treatment of urban villages....By March 2019, the government extended the policy to the entire city of Shenzhen through the 'Shenzhen Urban Village Integrated Rehabilitation Master Plan' (2019–2025)." Juan Du, *The Shenzhen Experiment: The Story of China's Instant City*, 2020, 306.

32 Du, *The Shenzhen Experiment*, 15.

33 Du, *The Shenzhen Experiment*, 16.

34 Joan Ockman, *Architecture Culture 1943–1968* (Columbia Books of Architecture, 1993), 408.

35 Paul Virilio, *The Oblique Function*. Originally published in February 1966, included in Ockman, *Architecture Culture 1943–1968*, 410.

36 The "environment" is referred to as in the same framework defined by EIC (Environment as the Integrating Context for Learning) advocates. Refer to: Lieberman and Hoody, *Closing the Achievement Gap*, 7.

37 A Vierendeel truss is a structure that does not utilize triangular members. The frame elements come together at fixed joints that are capable of transferring and resisting bending moments. We chose the Vierendeel truss for the bridges because of the following reasons: (a) it allows a seamless geometric continuity between the bridge and the vertical support elements, and (b) having no diagonal members within the frames allows better visual connectivity through the structure toward the banyan trees.

38 Spatial echoes here can also be read as the perspective-taking of the human-made toward the nature.

39 Author interviews with Early Learning Center teacher. Conducted by video conferencing on May 26, 2022.

40 Nietzsche had a mental breakdown in Turin, Italy. The incidence with the horse is an anecdote and there is no evidence that it truly happened.

41 Milan Kundera, *Unbearable of Lightness of Being* (Harper Perennial, 1999), 290.

42 Robin Evans, *The Projective Cast: Architecture and Its Three Geometries* (MIT Press, 1995), xxxi.

43 Paul Virilio, *The Oblique Function*. Originally published in February 1966, included in Ockman, *Architecture Culture 1943–1968*, 410.

44 Lieberman and Hoody, *Closing the Achievement Gap*, 7.

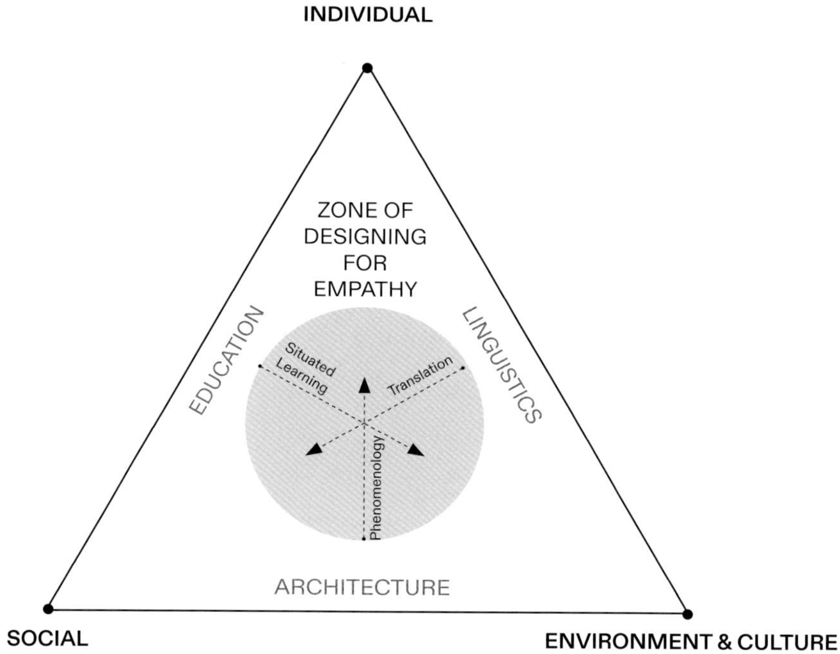
INDIVIDUAL
ZONE OF DESIGNING FOR EMPATHY
EDUCATION
LINGUISTICS
Situated Learning
Translation
Phenomenology
ARCHITECTURE
SOCIAL
ENVIRONMENT & CULTURE

6

CONCLUSION

After wandering through interdisciplinary ideas and architectural conjectures on designing for empathy, we should revisit the triangular map—the framework of the design explorations—presented in the first chapter.

In the discussion of development and empathy (refer to page 41), Dr. Higdon describes three vantage points: individual, social, and environment & culture. Education, linguistics, and architecture are the three key disciplines, overlaid on the edges in between the relevant vantage points. At the center of the triangle map, a zone is marked for "Designing for Empathy," to illustrate the conceptual links from each discipline to the design conjectures in this book.

For instance, in the 416 Memorial Park project (refer to page 110), the importance of translations is underlined between the meaning of balance as a land-borne concept and the perception of it during a maritime disaster. The constant negotiations at sea between the forces of buoyancy and gravity challenge the axes of our deictic center, and to understand the loss of balance between these forces, and the meaning of a tilt that is not correcting itself at sea, requires translation. The conceptual thread of the project is to create spatial translations where one language takes the perspective of another.

The "theory of learning as a dimension of social practice," as advocated by Lave and Wenger, recontextualizes schooling, and thus provides us another conceptual thread: education takes perspective of its context through situated learning.[1] For instance, at the Avenues Shenzhen campus, the purposefully designed interpenetrations between the school and the Tanglang urban village creates active engagement with the community and the environment. By negotiating the lines between itself and its context, the design strategies

6.1 Designing for Empathy Map

of the school, in a way, takes the perspective of the Tanglang urban village, which has evolved and sustained itself through constant negotiations between Shenzhen's fast growing urban fabric and its agrarian routes.

All the design examples in the book describe the concrete presence of spatial constructs as they relate to the experience of them—the phenomenological dimension of being in space. For instance, the three niches conjecture, that defines a clear perspectival space with conspicuous visual cues allow for reflections within the deictic depth. The intended experience is choreographed to nudge the children to take the perspective of the [other].

It is important to underline that encouraging perspective taking has been the central objective of the case studies in this book. Following the discussion on play and empathy, we can now state that the play drive is the agency of perspective taking. It is how we shift our cognitive and emotional awareness, and every design example discussed in this book, one way or another, activates our play drive. For instance, the children in the three niches conjecture (refer to page 91) are nudged to take the perspective of the other by shifting their deictic center. And they do that through playing with reflection in the perspectival depth. Or drift, as advocated by the Situationist International, is a form of imaginative play that has the potential to foster both individual exploration and social cohesion.[2] The spatial manifestation of drift is the "architecture of connections," which is not about connecting one point to another, but creating paths interwoven around spatial attractors, for encouraging spontaneous discovery.

This book itself is a manifestation of drift, as it wanders around intellectual attractors in the pursuit of designing for empathy. The premise of this approach is the collective rethinking of the learning environments, one that will inherently be more empathic as its spatial narratives are constructed through the interactions of its learners.

CONCLUSION
CHAPTER NOTES

1 Jean Lave and Étienne Wenger, *Situated Learning: Legitimate Peripheral Participation* (Cambridge University Press, 1991), 47.

2 For more information on Situationist International refer to Simon Sadler, *The Situationist City* (MIT Press, 1998).

ACKNOWLEDGMENTS

In fall 2016, I met William Lidwell and Liz Lee at Avenues World School Headquarters in New York City. That one meeting played a pivotal role in the following seven years of my design focus and, consequently, the creation of this book. I was inspired by their mission to transform how we learn. It resonated with my own mission to make a meaningful difference in people's lives through architecture, and I thought, what better way to do it than designing learning environments. I would like to thank Will and Liz for their inspiration, encouragement, and support on this journey. My work could not have come to fruition without the trust of Jeff Clark, the president of Avenues, and the support of Lloyd Nathan and Tom Gannon. I am grateful for the immersive collaboration we have had with Avenues World School across different campuses and everyone in the organization who we have worked with during the past seven years.

I would like to extend my thanks to:

> Dr. Julia Higdon, not only for her essay contribution to this book, but also for the workshops and discussions we had in the past two years. Her intellectual guidance on human development and empathy has been an invaluable support in my research.
>
> Dr. Lisa Landrum, Architecture Department Chair at Toronto Metropolitan University, for her peer review of the book.
>
> Julia van den Hout, my editor, for her diligence and guidance.
>
> Original Copy for the book design.
>
> Gordon Goff, Jake Anderson, and the team at Applied Research and Design for their support of this book.

This book is based on design research conducted with my team at Efficiency Lab for Architecture. I thank my colleagues for their commitment to Architecture's core mission as a humanist endeavor.

Efficiency Lab for Architecture team:
Yousef Abdul-Emir, Aybars Aşçı, Ashley Dotson, Maya Galbis, Miaoting He, Olivia Holub, Emilija Landsbergis, Love Liljeqvist, Christopher Olsen, Chas Peppers, Eda Şarman, Li Shao, Lara Steiner, Catherine Wilmes, Zheng Yin, Andrew Zelmer

(Facing page) Avenues Silicon Valley, Parent Information Center. Entrance to the multi-purpose room.

AUTHOR BIOGRAPHIES

Aybars Aşçı

Architect and educator Aybars Aşçı is an advocate of research-driven design, with a focus on designing learning environments. His projects range from planning large-scale campuses to designing play structures. As a practicing architect he has over 25 years of experience, working in New York and London, on projects located in North America, South America, Middle East, and Asia. As an educator, he has taught seminars and design studios at the City College of New York, Cornell University, Pratt Institute, and Northeastern University. As an inventor, he holds a U.S. patent for a high performance enclosure system (Patent #9003727; approved 4-14-2015).

Aşçı is the president and founder of Efficiency Lab for Architecture, a design practice based in New York.

He holds a Master of Science in Advanced Architectural Design from Columbia University.

Dr. Julia Higdon

Dr. Julia Higdon is a Senior Research Scientist on the Research & Development team at Avenues: The World School, where she and her team conduct original research on human development, global education, and organizational health. She received her doctorate in education from Harvard University Graduate School of Education.

Higdon is a co-author of *Empowering Global Citizens: A World Course* (CreateSpace Independent Publishing Platform, 2016), and *The Elements of Education for Teachers: 50 Research-based Principles Every Educator Should Know* (Routledge, 2019), among other publications.

IMAGE CREDITS

Images and drawings courtesy Aybars Aşçı and Efficiency Lab for Architecture unless otherwise noted.

Cover
Zhang Chao Architectural Photography

Introduction
4 Si Hu
10–13 Josh Johnson

Empathy in Perspective
40 NASA/JPL-Caltech

Deixis and Empathy
70 Blake Marvin
72 Zhang Chao Architectural Photography
76 Originally published in Robin Evans, *The Projective Cast: Architecture and Its Three Geometries* (MIT Press, 1995), 367.
78 Wouter Hagens, CC BY-SA 3.0
80 (top) Anthony McCall, *Line Describing a Cone*, 1973. Film projector, haze machine. Installation view at the Whitney Museum of Modern Art, 2001.
Photo: Hank Graber © Anthony McCall. Courtesy: the artist and Sean Kelly, New York/Los Angeles
(bottom) Installation Study, 2006. Graphite on paper © Anthony McCall. Courtesy: the artist and Sean Kelly, New York/Los Angeles
81 Albrecht Dürer, *Man Drawing a Lute*
90 Zhang Chao Architectural Photography
95 (top left) Raphael, *The School of Athens*
(top right) Photo by Lure
111 (top) Photo by The Republic of Korea Coast Guard via Getty Images

Movement and Empathy
124 Zhang Chao Architectural Photography
128 Leonardo Da Vinci, *Vitruvian Man,* Collection of the Gallerie dell'Accademia
129 Inessa Binenbaum & Efficiency Lab for Architecture
130–131 Inessa Binenbaum
133 Inessa Binenbaum & Efficiency Lab for Architecture
134 Inessa Binenbaum
135 SiTu
136 Inessa Binenbaum
137 Zhang Chao Architectural Photography
140 Constant, *New Babylon Noord.* Kunstmuseum Den Haag © Foto: Tom Haartsen
145 Originally published in John J. Fruin, "Designing for Pedestrians: A Level-of-Service Concept," 1971, pp. 7 (left) and 13 (right)
155 (left) Hema Maps
(right) den keck, CC0, via Wikimedia Commons
164 Zhang Chao Architectural Photography
166 (top right) Josh Hallett, CC BY-SA 2.0
168 (bottom) Julia van den Hout
171 Si Hu
173 Zhang Chao Architectural Photography
174 Zhang Chao Architectural Photography

Play and Empathy
180 Deborah Galhardi
185 The Drs. Nicholas and Dorothy Cummings Center for the History of Psychology, The University of Akron
191 Zhang Chao Architectural Photography
192–193 Zhang Chao Architectural Photography
194 Zhang Chao Architectural Photography
195 Si Hu
196–197 Si Hu
198 Si Hu
208 Si Hu
209 Si Hu
210 (left) Melikamp, CC BY-SA 3.0
211 Constant, *Klein Labyr.* Kunstmuseum Den Haag © Foto: Tom Haartsen
213 Si Hu
214–215 Si Hu

228 Blake Marvin

PROJECT CREDITS

Avenues Shenzhen Early Learning Center
Architecture: Efficiency Lab for Architecture
Interior Design: Efficiency Lab for Architecture
Landscape Design: Terrain
Structural Design: SOM – Structure
Local Design Institute: CCDI
Local Design Coordinator: Wei Wei
Lighting Design: Claude Engel
Acoustic Design: WSDG
Project Management: Arcadis
Cost Estimator: RLB
Contractor: EDG

Avenues Shenzhen Primary School
Architecture: Efficiency Lab for Architecture
Interior Design: Efficiency Lab for Architecture
Landscape Design: WAY Design
Structural Design: ARUP
Local Design Institute: CCDI
Facade Consultant: Inhabit
Lighting Design: Claude Engel
Acoustic Design: Longman Lindsey
Kitchen Consultant: Ricca Design Studios
Project Management: Arcadis
Contractor: Kingon

Avenues Shenzhen Master Plan
Master Plan: Efficiency Lab for Architecture
Architecture: Efficiency Lab for Architecture
Local Planning Institute: Shenzhen Urban Planning Institute
Local Design Institute: CCDI
Local Design Coordinator: Wei Wei

Avenues Silicon Valley Campus
Master Plan: Efficiency Lab for Architecture
Architecture: Efficiency Lab for Architecture
Land Use: The Morley Bros.
Local Architect of Record: Adamson Associates
Structural Design: SOM – Structure
MEP/AV/IT/Security: Syska Hennessy
Civil Engineer: Kimley-Horn
Traffic: Hexagon
Fire Engineering: Holmes
Environmental: David J. Powers
Lighting Design: Claude Engel
Landscape Design: Bionic
Cost Estimator: RLB

Avenues Silicon Valley—Parent Information Center
Architecture: Efficiency Lab for Architecture
Interior Design: Efficiency Lab for Architecture
Local Architect of Record: Adamson Associates
Structural Design: SOM – Structure
MEP/AV/IT/Security: Syska Hennessy
Lighting Design: Claude Engel
Acoustic Design: Longman Lindsey
Civil Engineer: Kimley-Horn
Cost Estimator: RLB
Project Manager: Kitchell
Contractor: Turner

Avenues Miami Campus
Master Plan: Efficiency Lab for Architecture
Architecture: Efficiency Lab for Architecture
Landuse Consultant: Greenberg Traurig
Local Architect of Record: Zyscovich
Civil & Traffic Engineering: Langan
MEP: TLC
AV/IT/Security: Syska Hennessy
Landscape Design: Savino Miller
Arborist: Lisa Hammer
Cost: Gardiner & Theobald
Pre-construction: Turner

Avenues Miami—Community Information Center
Architecture: Efficiency Lab for Architecture
Interior Design: Efficiency Lab for Architecture
Local Architect of Record: Zyscovich
Structural Design: Thornton Tomasetti
Landscape Design: Savino Miller
Arborist: Lisa Hammer
Civil Engineering: Langan
Landscape Design: Savino Miller
MEP/AV/IT/Security: Syska Hennessy
Lighting Design: Tillotson

PROJECT CREDITS

Acoustic Design: Longman Lindsey
Kitchen: Ricca Design Studios
Cost: RLB
Pre-construction: Turner

Avenues New York Small World
Architecture: Efficiency Lab for Architecture
Interior Design: Efficiency Lab for Architecture
Lighting Design: Claude Engel
Acoustic Design: Longman Lindsey
MEP: TWIG
Code & Accessibility: CCI
Expeditor: Millrose
General Contractor: Taurino Management
Playscape Contractor: Situ Fabrication

Avenues São Paulo Campus—Phase 2
Architecture & Planning: Efficiency Lab for Architecture
Landscape Design: Terrain
Structural Engineer: Certiphic

Telluride Glass House
Architecture: Efficiency Lab for Architecture
Local Architect of Record: Tommy Hein
Interior Design: Gachot Studios
Structural Design: SOM – Structure
MEP: Bighorn Consulting Engineers
Civil Engineer: Uncompahgre Engineering
Geo-Hazard Engineer: Trautner Geotech
Contractor: Finbro Construction

Senegal Elementary School
Architecture: Efficiency Lab for Architecture
Structural Engineer: NY Engineering

Doha Art Pavilion
Architecture: Efficiency Lab for Architecture
Interior Design: Efficiency Lab for Architecture
Local Architect of Record: AEB
Structural Design: LERA
Enclosure: Eckersley O'Callaghan
Project Management: Hill International

Kaunas Concert Hall
Architecture: Efficiency Lab for Architecture

LIMA Art Museum New Contemporary Art Wing
Architecture: Efficiency Lab for Architecture

Berlin Wall Enclosure
Architecture: Efficiency Lab for Architecture

416 Memorial Park
Architecture: Efficiency Lab for Architecture

PK-8 Campus—US Virgin Islands
Architecture: Efficiency Lab for Architecture

INDEX

INDEX

Published by Applied Research and Design Publishing, an imprint of ORO Editions.
Gordon Goff: Publisher

www.appliedresearchanddesign.com
info@appliedresearchanddesign.com

Editor: Julia van den Hout
Author: Aybars Aşçı
Book Design: Original Copy
Project Manager: Jake Anderson

10 9 8 7 6 5 4 3 2 1 First Edition

ISBN: 978-1-957183-42-8

Color Separations and Printing: ORO Editions Inc.
Printed in China

AR+D Publishing makes a continuous effort to minimize the overall carbon footprint of its publications. As part of this goal, AR+D, in association with Global ReLeaf, arranges to plant trees to replace those used in the manufacturing of the paper produced for its books. Global ReLeaf is an international campaign run by American Forests, one of the world's oldest nonprofit conservation organizations. Global ReLeaf is American Forests' education and action program that helps individuals, organizations, agencies, and corporations improve the local and global environment by planting and caring for trees.